Marital and Family Therapy

Marital and Family Therapy

Ira D. Glick, M.D.

*Associate Professor of Psychiatry
in Residence
University of California School of Medicine,
San Francisco, California;
Career Teacher in Psychiatry
of the National Institute of Mental Health*

David R. Kessler, M.D.

*Associate Clinical Professor of Psychiatry,
University of California School of Medicine,
San Francisco;
Director, Crisis Intervention Unit,
Langley Porter Neuropsychiatric Institute,
San Francisco, California*

With a Foreword by Theodore Lidz, M.D.
*Professor of Psychiatry,
Yale University School of Medicine,
New Haven, Connecticut*

GRUNE & STRATTON
A Subsidiary of Harcourt Brace Jovanovich, Publishers
New York   San Francisco   London

Library of Congress Cataloging in Publication Data

Glick, Ira D   1937-
    Marriage and family therapy.

    Includes bibliographical references.
        1. Family psychotherapy.   I. Kessler, David R.,
joint author.   II. Title.   [DNLM: 1. Family.
2. Family therapy. 3. Marriage.   WM430 G559m]
RC488.5.G54   616.8'915   74-19236
ISBM 0-8089-0854-5

Grune & Stratton, Inc.
111 Fifth Avenue
New York, New York 10003

Library of Congress Catalog Card Number 74-13366
International Standard Book Number 0-8089-0843-X
Printed in the United States of America

To our Families

Contents

Tables and Figures

Foreword

I have been given the unusual opportunity of welcoming a book which, I believe, is the first proper text in a relatively new field, an opportunity I welcome, for I can recommend the book with enthusiasm to the many students in the various helping professions who have need for it and to their teachers whose task it will lighten. It is written clearly and concisely, and with a deceptive simplicity that reflects the authors' mastery of the topic, the orderliness of their minds, and an awareness of what students need to know and what they can assimilate without extensive clinical experience.

The preparation of the first text presents its authors with formidable problems of assembling material, organization, selection of topics, and so forth, without the opportunity to lean upon earlier authors and to crib from them. There have been, of course, other books about family and marital therapy. Nathan Ackerman's *Treating the Troubled Family* and Virginia Satir's *Conjoint Family Therapy* have both served as guides to many, but both were written by pioneers and innovators and both advanced primarily the author's own views and techniques. Here, in contrast, we are offered a balanced and carefully planned approach. I found myself admiring the method of presentation, the selection of what to include, and the authors' ability to remember that they were writing an introductory text and to forego the narcissistic gratifications of displaying their consummate knowledge of the field.

I have read and reread the manuscript with pleasure as well as benefit. Even though I have followed the field of family therapy since its inception, the book clarified various salient issues for me and set differing therapeutic techniques in perspective. Some readers, probably more teachers than students, may consider the approach conservative. It does not promulgate innovative concepts or techniques; its creativity derives from the sorting out of diverse approaches introduced by persons of divergent training, ideologies, and personalities, and integrating them into a coherent presentation. The conservativism is not only appropriate in an introductory text, but also needed in this new therapeutic field in which there has been a plethora of innovative techniques, some of which have been impractical, some unbridled, and some highly manipulative. Therapists have often impatiently sought shortcuts in promoting changes in personality functioning through changing family transactions without adequate appreciation of the strong forces that foster pattern maintenance in the family.

The authors properly do not consider methods and techniques alone, but seek to establish an adequate foundation in family structure and dynamics for the future therapist. They recognize that the family not only forms a true small group in which the action of any member affects all, but that it has very special characteristics because of the prolonged and intense relationships between its members; because it is divided into two generations and two sexes; and because of the interrelated functions it serves for the couple who marry, for the children born into it, and for the society in which it exists. Although a marital or family therapist requires substantial knowledge of personality development and functioning on the one hand, and of larger social systems on the other, the authors confine themselves, as they must, to marriage and the family and assume that the student will have gained such knowledge elsewhere.

The authors, I was pleased to find, take a broad view of marital and family therapy, rather than limit themselves to the consideration of conjoint therapy. Taken in the broadest sense, family therapy can include any form of treatment that takes the import and impact of family transactions into account when considering the etiology and treatment of personality disorders. Only one person, the patient, a parent, or a spouse may be in actual treatment, but the focus is upon changing the family interaction; or, the various members of the family may each be treated individually; or all members of the family may be seen together in a group together with members of other families. However, the focus of the book is, as it should be, primarily on conjoint family therapy. When it is preferable to work with the designated patient and his internalizations of family members, when with the family or marital partner conjointly, and when with multiple couples or families in a group requires careful judgment and the authors offer judicious, nondogmatic opinions that provide guidance for reaching such decisions.

The authors review the more widely used and most widely promulgated of the many different types of family therapy that have emerged, but rather than giving lengthly descriptions of a variety of techniques or promoting one above the other, they sensibly seek to instruct the student in three basic therapeutic strategies: the facilitation of communication of thoughts and feelings between family members; the attempt to shift disturbed, inflexible roles and coalitions; and the therapist's use of himself or herself as a family role model, educator, and demythologizer. Family therapy is a difficult therapeutic technique that has all too often been undertaken by persons with little, if any, experience in working with individuals or with meaningful groups. The inexperienced therapist can inadvertently promote disorganization of an individual or of a family because of his countertransference to a family member, his transference of his own family problems into the situation, his exasperation with the rigidities or lack of empathy of family members, his shock at the cruelties that may go on within a family, his narcissistic needs, or simply by lack of recognition of his own limitations, as well as in still other ways. The book recognizes that any form of therapy that can promote significant change in the individual or family can also misfire and cause harm. It provides the basic knowledge the future therapist needs before entering into supervised work with couples or families, and emphasizes the importance of supervised clinical experience in addition to didactic instruction. The field as a whole, as well as those entering it, will be benefited greatly by this well-tempered work, and I confidently predict that it will enjoy a wide readership, a long life, and many future editions as the field advances.

Theodore Lidz, M.D.
Professor of Psychiatry,
Yale University School of Medicine,
New Haven, Connecticut

Preface

Marital and family therapy have evolved so rapidly, from their inception 15 years ago, that practitioners and teachers have "future shock."[1] What seemed standard then, seems questionable now. It seems appropriate, therefore, to summarize our knowledge of theory and techniques in the field at this time, and to offer beginning students an introductory textbook that will provide some overall fundamentals on which to build. Our hope is (1) to present some of the core concepts relevant to an understanding of families; (2) to offer a frame of reference for planning and carrying out family therapy strategies; and (3) to summarize some current research on family process and treatment.

We have found, in teaching about marital and family therapy, that certain questions are asked repeatedly, such as: How does family therapy compare with other psychotherapies in theory, technique, and results? What kinds of family situations do best with family therapy, and which present serious obstacles? What kinds of change can be expected in individuals and in family systems as a result of family therapy? We think the reader of this book will develop some understanding of the issues raised by these questions.

This book is intended for beginning students in a variety of professional helping disciplines, including psychiatry, medicine, psychology, social work, the ministry, law, corrections, education, and others. Marital and family problems are major aspects of the work in such fields, and some knowledge of and experience with the basic principles of dealing with them should help promote increased competence and confidence.

In this book we have tried to present some of the major principles of the field. To accomplish this, we have selectively distilled a few basic elements from a large and, at times, untidy pool of ideas. While we have tried to focus on those concepts relating most specifically to a family systems framework, we have included also other models where these seem conceptually and practically useful.

Our intention is to educate rather than to advocate. Clearly, the ideas presented here are those we feel will be most useful to a beginner in the field, but their inclusion, to the exclusion of others, should not be interpreted as a fixed, final, qualitative assessment. Rather, we hope the family therapist will utilize the concepts presented herein as a point of departure and growth. Education is the process that helps the student to practice better family therapy, and information is a tool. It is the therapist who will use his sense organs to detect the cries of distress and, in time, will arrive at the personal amalgam of concepts and techniques that seem most viable to him.[2]

We realize that a textbook alone will not suffice to give a complete picture of what family therapy is. There is, obviously, no substitute for observing and working with actual families in trouble. Such experience cannot be easily or thoroughly communicated in print. For this reason, among others, we have omitted verbal transcripts of family therapy sessions. These are available elsewhere,[3-7] as are films dealing with family therapy.[8-10] Nevertheless, the complexity and nonverbal aspects of the interactions do not often come through to the reader from the printed page. We hope that what is offered here will equip the beginning family worker to feel more competent and comfortable in observing, understanding, and treating those families who need his help.

Finally, a word of caution. Marital and family treatment are relatively new techniques. This entire field is in its infancy. Therefore, despite the humanism, strong enthusiasm, and conviction of workers in the field, students should be scientifically skeptical regarding the diverse basic hypotheses of family therapy and evaluation of its methods and results.

We do not claim any blinding originality for this book. We have, indeed, unashamedly borrowed extensively from our teachers, our colleagues, and our students. But we take full responsibility for having organized and selected the materials presented.

REFERENCES

1. Toffler A: Future Shock. New York, Random House, 1970.
2. Ingelfinger F: Advertising: Informational but not educational. N Engl J Med 286:1319, 1972.

3. Haley J, Hoffman L: Techniques of Family Therapy. New York, Basic Books, 1967.
4. Ackerman N W (ed): Family Therapy in Transition. Boston, Little, Brown, 1970.
5. Watzlawick P J: An Anthology of Human Communication. Palo Alto, Ca, Science and Behavior Books, 1964.
6. Zuk G: Family Therapy: A Triadic Based Approach. New York, Behavioral Publications, 1971.
7. Sager C, Brayboy T, Waxenberg B: Black Ghetto Family in Therapy: A Laboratory Experience. New York, Grove Press, 1970.
8. The Enemy and Myself. 16mm Black and White Sound Film, 50 min., by N Ackerman, M.D. (The Family Institute, New York, NY 10021).
9. Family Therapy: An Introduction. 16mm Black and White Sound Film, 43 min., by Ira D. Glick, M.D. (University of California Medical Center, San Francisco, Ca 94143) and George J. Marshall, Sr. (Medical College of Georgia, Augusta, Ga. 30904).
10. Family in Crisis. 16mm Color Sound Film 48 min., by David R. Kessler, M.D. (Langley Porter Neuropsychiatric Institute, University of California San Francisco Medical Center, San Francisco, Ca. 94143).

Acknowledgments

We wish to thank a variety of individuals and families who have helped to make this book possible:

First, our own families of origin, who in addition to steadfastly attempting to socialize us, provided us with our first major models of family structure and function. Second, our teachers, Theodore Lidz and Thomas Detre at the Yale University Department of Psychiatry; Irwin Greenberg at Hillside Hospital, New York City; and Alan Leveton at the Mt. Zion Hospital, San Francisco, who by their interest and enthusiasm first helped to stir our interest in family study and treatment and provided us with a family model of understanding human functioning. Third, our colleagues in family therapy, especially Henry Lennard and Jay Haley, who by their stimulating and provocative comments, tried their best to keep us honest. Fourth, our trainees, with whom we have been privileged to work on the teaching-learning process in family therapy. It is they who have had the courage to ask the critical questions about the field, and it was for them that much of the didactic material in this textbook was formulated and used in courses we have taught both here and at other institutions.

Finally, a special word of thanks to those of our students and colleagues who took the time to read and comment on what was then a fairly raw first draft, and who offered invaluable critical comments and suggestions for change. They include Dan Dinaburg, Leon Epstein, Stephen Fleck, Jay Haley, Jacob Katzow, Alan Leveton, Michael Peterson, Donald Ransom, and Carlos Sluzki. We are indebted to Patricia T.

Kelly, Ph. D., for suggestions for the section on family and genetic counseling and to Harvey S. Kaplan, M. D., for suggestions for the section on
family and child abuse. Of course, we take sole responsibility for the end
results. In addition, a number of people helped in preparing the manuscript. They include Ms. Judi Yabamoto, Barbara Lee, and Mary Har-
greaves who patiently typed the drafts of the manuscript, Mr. Jon Showstack for a variety of assistance, Ms. Margo Showstack for her help in
preparing the index, and Ms. Mary Ann Esser for valuable work in
editing the manuscript. In addition, special thanks are due to the United
States Public Health Service for support of Dr. Glick from July, 1971, to
June, 1973, when he was a Career Teacher of the National Institute of
Mental Health, MH-12450, and spent part of that time working on this
book.

Most of all, we are indebted to the families whom we have treated.
They have patently demonstrated the complexity of individual and family
functioning and made it obvious that problems of families do not fit neatly
into any one theoretical framework.

Marital and Family Therapy

1

The Field of Marital
and Family Treatment:
Development and Definition

OBJECTIVES

- To understand the historical development of family therapy
- To define what family therapy is (and what it is not)

Although the fields of marital and family treatment* are relatively young, there is nothing particularly new about the general significance of marriage and the family. It probably does not require any specific training or knowledge to perceive that these are important human systems, and that they are different in several essential ways from other types of human groups and relationships.

Since World War II, the number of families in the United States increased by about 12,000,000 in 18 years, to 47,800,000 in March, 1965, and is expected another 14,000,000 in the next fifteen years . . . The married couples responsible for the usual concept of family life will number 55,200,000 by 1980.

Living thus together as members of families there were [1965] some 177,600,000 persons, or 92 percent of the population. More than 41,600,000 of these individuals were the heads of husband-wife families, responsible for a total of some 55,800,000 children under fourteen years of age, and many older ones.

*To avoid unnecessary duplication, the phrase "family treatment" (for "family system," "family unit") will be used in this book from this point on, and is to be understood to mean *marital and family* treatment (system, or unit) except where specifically otherwise indicated.

Seven out of every eight families are headed by a husband whose wife is living and domiciled at least part of the day at home. Ten per cent of families have a woman as the head, either widowed or divorced, but often responsible for the support as well as the physical, moral, and social care and training of her children.[1]

Most people would be likely to agree that marriages and families perform vital tasks for the individuals involved in them, and for society at large. It has long been a commonsense view that we are all shaped in major ways as human beings by what we have experienced in our original families, and that what occurs in our current marital or family system is, for most people, the prime element in our general sense of well-being and functioning.

Clearly, individual family units are different from one another, and some function "better" or are "happier" than others. Many helping professionals in the past two decades have begun to examine more closely the processes and circumstances that lead to family distress and to attempt to devise means by which the distress might be alleviated. The following chapters will discuss some basic concepts and techniques associated with family therapy. At this point, however, we will offer a brief review of the emergence of this field, followed by a delineation of its scope.

DEVELOPMENT OF THE FAMILY THERAPY FIELD

Although exciting, innovative, and seemingly useful in helping families with problems in living, family therapy can, at times, be confusing to the beginner. It is hard to understand the fundamentals of the field and to differentiate them from individual styles of charismatic therapists, as well as to synthesize divergent theories from different fields such as psychology, psychiatry, sociology, psychoanalysis, game theory, communication theory, Gestalt therapy, and the like. How did this state of affairs come about?

The importance attributed to the family's role in relation to the psychic and social distress of any of its members has waxed and waned over many years. The important role of the family in the development of individual problems was mentioned by Confucius and in the Greek myths. The early Hawaiians would meet as a family to discuss solutions whenever a problem came up with an individual.

For a long time in our own culture, however, what we now call mental illness and other forms of interpersonal distress were ascribed to magical, religious, physical, or exclusively intrapersonal factors. At the turn of this century, Freud attempted to elucidate individual psychodynamics as determinants of human behavior. Although he stressed the major role of the family in the development of individual symptoms, he believed that the most effective technique for dealing with such individual psychopathology was treatment on a one-to-one basis. At about the same time, others began to suggest that families with a sick member should be seen together—not "as individuals removed from family relationships" (p. 377).[2] The importance of dealing with the family unit was recognized in child guidance clinics from the first half of this century, where psychiatric social workers often saw one or both parents individually or jointly.

In the 1930s a psychoanalyst reported his experience in treating a marital pair.[3] In the 1940s, Fromm-Reichmann[4] postulated that a pathologic mother (called the "schizophrenogenic mother") can induce schizophrenia in a "vulnerable" child. This speculation led other psychoanalysts, such as Lidz,[5] to study the role of the father. This work suggested that the father also plays an important role in development of psychopathology. At the same time, Mittelman[6] began to see a series of marital partners in simultaneous, but separate, psychoanalyses. This was quite innovative, because previous beliefs held that this would hinder rather than help the therapist, and the marital partner usually was referred to a colleague. It was thought that neither spouse could trust the therapist and would hold back important material.

Outside the field of psychiatry proper, marital counselors, ministers, and others had been interviewing spouses together for some time. Apparently it was in the early 1950s that the first consistent use of family therapy in modern psychotherapeutic practice in the United States was reported by several different workers.[6,7] Ackerman[8] began consistently utilizing family interviews in his work with children and adolescents in the 1950s. At about this same time, Lidz et al.[9] and Bowen[10] began a more extensive series of investigations of family interactions and schizophrenia. Bateson et al.[11] and Wynne et al.[12] began the more intensive study of family communication patterns in the families of schizophrenic patients and others.

However, it was not until the early 1960s that these ideas were integrated into a general theory of family interrelationships, and the field of family therapy began to take shape.[8,13] Various schools of thought developed. Journals were established, such as *Family Process*. Many people became interested in learning about and doing family therapy.

Still, as we are well into the 1970s, family therapy is a relatively new field compared to individual psychotherapy and psychopharmacotherapy. As yet, hypotheses and results, although enthusiastically supported, are but thinly documented. Only recently has more controlled research begun on what actually transpires in families[14,15] and on the outcome of family therapy.[16,17] To some extent, these same difficulties apply to most other psychosocial treatments in psychiatry (which do, however, have a greater backlog of clinical experience and acceptance behind them). Further discussion of research into family process and family treatment will be found in Chapters 13 and 14.

DEFINITION

Marital and family treatment can be defined as a professionally organized attempt to produce beneficial changes in a disturbed marital or family unit by essentially interactional, nonphysical methods. Its aim is the establishment of more satisfying ways of living for the entire family, and not only for a single family member.

Family therapy is distinguished from other psychotherapies by its conceptual focus on the family system as a whole. In this view, major emphasis is placed on understanding individual behavior patterns as arising from and inevitably feeding back into the complicated matrix of the general family system. Beneficial alterations in the larger marital and family unit will, therefore, have positive consequences for the individual members, as well as for the larger system. The major emphasis is placed upon understanding and intervening in the family system's current patterns of interaction, with usually only a secondary interest in their origins and development.

One family member may be "selected" as the "symptom bearer." He will then be described in a variety of ways that amount to his being either "bad, sick, stupid, or crazy." Depending on what sort of label this individual carries, he, together with his family, may be seen in any one of several types of helping facility—psychiatric, correctional, medical.

On the other hand, there may not always be an "identified patient." Occasionally, a marital or family unit presents itself as being in trouble without singling out any one member. A marital couple may realize that their marriage is in trouble and that it is their interaction, rather than anything about either one of them alone, that seems to be creating problems.

There is a continuum between the so-called intrapsychic system, the interactional family system, and the sociocultural system. Different conceptual frameworks are utilized when dealing with these systems. A therapist may choose to place his emphasis at any point on this continuum; the family therapist is especially sensitive to and trained in those aspects relating specifically to the family system.

This family system viewpoint is especially useful in certain kinds of situations in which the family resists change (see Chapter 10). Family therapy is designed to deal with situations that are seen primarily as interfering in the family system as a whole or in marital or parent-child relationships. On the other hand, a greater amount of emphasis on the individual intrapsychic factors may be more practical in other kinds of families (see Chapter 11). Individual psychotherapy is, for example, designed to help an individual live better with himself. Other types of treatment may be appropriate under still other conditions, for example, group therapy may be particularly indicated for those who suffer from inadequate, nongratifying social relationships with peers (Table 1).

The question is often asked, "Do individuals in the family system change their personality structure as a result of family therapy?" Without going into the question of whether individuals *can* change their personalities, family therapy attempts to change family interaction, structure, and function. As a result of such change, certain aspects of the personality of an individual may change. In general, then, family therapy does not have a primary goal of changing underlying personality structure in isolation from its relationship to the family context.

Family therapy is not necessarily synonomous with *conjoint family therapy* (in which the entire family meets together consistently for therapy sessions). There are instances in which a family may be seen together, but the therapist's frame of reference is that of individual psychotherapy. Family members in such a setting may be treated as relatively isolated individual entities. In effect, then, such a therapist may be doing individual psychotherapy in the usual family therapy setting, and without the frame of reference of the family system as a whole.

On the other hand, instead of having regular sessions with the entire family, one of the clinical and theoretical pioneers in the family field has in recent years been utilizing mainly or exclusively the "healthiest member" of the family system as his therapeutic agent for change in the family unit. This same therapist has also reported on the use of somewhat indirect means, such as provocative letters to family members, as an imaginative way to conduct family therapy, that is, to bring about change or movement in a family system.[18]

Family therapy might broadly be thought of as any type of psychosocial intervention utilizing a conceptual framework that gives primary emphasis to the family system, and which in its therapeutic strategies aims for an impact on the entire family structure. Thus, any psychotherapeutic approach that attempts to understand or to intervene in an organically-viewed family system might fittingly be called *family therapy.* This is a very broad definition and allows many competing points of view, both in theory and in therapy, to be placed under one heading.

Although many clinicians agree that there is faulty interaction in families containing an individual with gross disturbance, it is not always clear whether the faulty interaction is cause or effect. These two points of view were summarized by the Group for the Advancement of Psychiatry[19] in 1970:

Table 1
Family Therapy Compared with Other Types of Psychosocial Therapy

Type	Goals	Focus	Role of Therapist	Major Indications	Participants	Length and Frequency of Sessions	Overall Duration of Treatment
FAMILY THERAPY	Improved family functioning	Family communication; coalition and roles	Active, participant-observer	Marital and parent-child problems	1 family unit, 1–2 therapists	1 1/2 hours, 1X/week	6 months–2 years
INDIVIDUAL PSYCHOTHERAPY Psycho-analysis	Personality restructuring	Past Unconscious Transference	Passive, nondirective	Unconscious conflicts in intact personality	1 patient 1 therapist	1 hour, 5X/week	2–5 years

Psychoanalytically-oriented psychotherapy	Personality modification	Present coping mechanisms	Active, participant-observer	Maladaptive pattern of defenses	1 patient 1 therapist	1 hour, 1–2X/week	6 months–2 years
Brief psychotherapy	Symptom removal	Restoration of functioning	Directive, suppressive	Disruption related to acute gross stress	1 patient 1 therapist	1hour, 1X/week	1–10 weeks
GROUP PSYCHOTHERAPY (e.g., analytic; encounter; marathon; psychodrama)	Improved social functioning	Group participation and feedback	Variable	Poor peer-group relationships	6–8 patients 1–2 therapists	1 1/2 hours, 1X/week	6 months–2 years
MILIEU THERAPY (e.g., "therapeutic communities"; day care centers)	Major modification of social behavior	Corrective social experience	Active, participant-observer	Pathogenic social environment	10–30 patients 10–30 staff	Residential (full or part-time)	3 months–2 years

Some practitioners continue to perceive and treat as the central issue . . . the disequilibrium in the intrapsychic apparatus of the [individual], viewing the contextual social matrix of development and adaptation and most particularly the family as adding an important dimension to their conceptualization and treatment. Others see and treat as the central issue the disequilibrium in the family, viewing the altered balance of intrapsychic forces and counterforces in an individual to be of secondary of or even of inconsequential relevance to the task of the helping professional (p. 534).

For the present, there is no reason to believe that both views may not be important. Pending further research and experience in this area, it would seem prudent to evaluate each clinical situation carefully, attempting both to understand the phenomena and to select intervention strategies designed to achieve the desired ends.

REFERENCES

1. Family life in America (Editorial). N Engl J Med 274:1209, 1966.
2. Smith Z E: Discussion on charity organizations. Proceedings of the National Conference on Charities and Correction, 1890, p. 377.
3. Oberndorf, C P: Folie à deaux. Int J Psychoanal 15:14–24, 1934.
4. Fromm-Reichmann F: Notes on the development of schizophrenia by psychoanalytic psychotherapy. Psychiatry 11:267–277, 1948.
5. Lidz R, Lidz T: The family environment of schizophrenic patients. Am J Psychiatry 106:322–345, 1949.
6. Mittelman B: The concurrent analysis of married couples. Psychoanal Q 17:182–197, 1948.
7. Bell J E: Family Group Therapy. Public Health Monograph No. 64. Washington, D. C.: Department of Health, Education and Welfare, Public Health Service, 1961.
8. Ackerman N W: Treating the Troubled Family. New York, Basic Books, 1966.
9. Lidz T, Cornelison A, Terry D, Fleck S: Intrafamilial environment of the schizophrenic patient. VI. The transmission of irrationality. Archives of Neurology and Psychiatry 79:305–316, 1958.
10. Bowen M: A family concept of schizophrenia, in Jackson D D (ed): The Etiology of Schizophrenia. New York, Basic Books, 1960, pp 346–372
11. Bateson G, Jackson D D, Haley J, Weakland J: Towards a theory of schizophrenia. Behav Sci 1:251–264, 1956.
12. Wynne L, Ryckoff I, Day J, Hersch S: Pseudo-mutuality in the family relations of schizophrenics. Psychiatry 21:205–220, 1958.
13. Satir V M: Conjoint Family Therapy: A Guide to Theory and Technique. Palo Alto, Ca, Science and Behavior Books, 1964.
14. Reiss, D: Individual thinking and family interaction. III. An experimental study of categorization performance in families of normals, those with character disorders, and schizophrenics. J Ner Ment Dis 146:384–404, 1968.

15. Reiss D: Individual thinking and family interaction. IV. A study of information exchange in families of normals, those with character disorders, and schizophrenics. J Ner Ment Dis 149:473–490, 1969.
16. Fitzgerald R V: Conjoint marital psychotherapy: An outcome and follow-up study. Family Process 8:261–271, 1969.
17. Wells R, Dilkes N, Trivelli N: The results of family therapy: A critical review of the literature. Family Process 11:189–208, 1972.
18. Towards the differentiation of a self in one's own family, in Framo J L (ed): Family Interaction: A Dialogue between Family Researchers and Family Therapists. New York, Springer, 1972, 111–166.
19. Group for the Advancement of Psychiatry. The Field of Family Therapy. Report No. 78. New York, Group for the Advancement of Psychiatry, 1970.

2

Understanding the Family

OBJECTIVES

- To understand the concept of the family as a system
- To list and characterize the phases of the family life cycle
- To list and understand primary family functions and tasks

There is probably little need to stress in great detail the general importance of the family and of marriage. These institutions have existed throughout recorded history in all places and all times. Even now, in late twentieth century America, despite the talk in some quarters about the "death of the family," family and marital relationships, although changing, are clearly very much with us and undoubtedly will continue to be so into the foreseeable future. Well over 90 percent of all people in the United States still live in families[1] and other than in early adulthood, human beings live in families most of their life.

However, it is certainly also true that marriage and the family have at various places and times carried different assignments and expectations, and this sort of variability appears to be very much in evidence in our present culture. Thus, while there still seem to be many examples of the "traditional American family," at the opposite extreme are all types of more or less radical approaches and modifications of this pattern. While the lack of a generally accepted pattern or standard for marriage and the family today is on the one hand a cause of uncertainty, instability, and distress, on the other, it provides for a multiplicity and richness of solutions for both individual and societal situations that a more rigid, unchanging pattern would not provide.

Birdwhistell[2] has suggested that the American family is organized around idealized, nonachievable goals (for example, romantic love). Failure to live up to such family myths (see Chapter 3) is a cause of great conflict and distress for all family members. Other writers also have questioned the validity of the "average, functional, normal" family and have pointed to the great diversity of family types and styles related to a variety of demographic and psychological variables. All families have conflicts, their feelings toward each other are mixed, their love is not always constant, and so forth. Furthermore, the completely well functioning, growing, long-term marriage is a rarity.

The frame of reference provided below for understanding the family is not intended to be exhaustive or complete. In our present state of understanding, no such final statement can be made. This model is intended to be supplementary to those frames of reference that apply to individual and sociocultural models. Their exclusion is not meant to imply that they are not important, but is in keeping with the general tenor of this book in presenting ideas of particular interest to the family therapist. It undoubtedly will be found that the richness, complexity, and variety of marriages and families will not be completely described or explained by the categories listed below, nor will all of the categories fit precisely into every specific family system. It is hoped, however, that the material presented below will offer a useful structure for thinking about all families, including those in distress who present themselves in one way or another to professionals for help.

THE FAMILY AS A SYSTEM

Marriage and the family are important human institutions, different from other human groups in many ways, including duration, intensity, and type of function. For most human beings, marriage and the family constitute the most important system, or group, in relation to individual psychological development, emotional interaction, and maintenance of self-esteem. For most of us, the family is the group in which we experience our strongest loves and our strongest hates, in which we enjoy our deepest satisfaction and suffer our most painful disappointments.

The characteristics of the family or of marriage as a unit are different from the mere sum of its component parts. Knowing the attributes of all the individuals in the family is not the same as understanding the family system as an entity. The family has a history and functions of its own, the specifics of which differ from those of its individual members.

Marriages and families need to be thought of as interactive milieus in which transactions between component parts are continually taking place. Thus, the action of any one member will affect the entire family. A ripple set up anywhere internally or externally that impinges on the family will reverberate throughout. There is a basic, underlying, consistent homeostasis in each family that is used to maintain each member's identity,[3] defined as the sum total of the individual's internal and external patterns of adjustment to life.[4] The family is a system in dynamic equilibrium. Stresses and strains of family existence inevitably affect each family member. At times, these reactions may be of such a nature as to cause them to be labeled as symptoms. For example, when a father and mother stop communicating (a change in homeostasis), the father may begin to drink (a symptom) or the mother may become depressed (a symptom).

The family usually is bound together by intense and long-lasting ties of past experience, social roles, mutual support, and expectations. Factors are constantly at work, more or less successfully, to keep the family system in equilibrium and to keep it from undergoing too severe or rapid change. This, too, has been referred to as family homeostasis. These equilibrating mechanisms often have to do with maintaining a continuing system of symmetrical and complementary relationships.

Family homeostasis refers most generally to the concept of the family as a feedback system designed, among other things, to maintain a relatively stable state, so that when the whole system or any part of it is subjected to a disequilibrating force, the system will operate to restore the preexisting equilibrium. Family therapists have noted that changes in one member of the family often bring about changes in other members. For instance, the onset of illness in the identified patient (for example, a child becomes schizophrenic) can cause others (mother) to decompensate (become depressed). As the child improves, the mother improves, and, concurrently, the father may become agitated.

Families can be thought of as having personalities or styles, analogous to those of individuals. A generally accepted system of family typologies is not available (though badly needed), but there is a general recognition of differences in family patterns of thinking, feeling, and interacting, of the types of coping mechanisms used to deal with stress, and the kinds of "myths" or "scripts" that families seem to act out. All marriages and families are subject to stress, disequilibrium, and crisis, and they all develop a greater or lesser number of habitual techniques with which they more or less successfully deal with these situtations.

While stability and homeostasis are important elements of marital and family systems, inevitably there are forces that are continually changing the family, pushing it in the direction of development and differentiation. Some of these forces constitute the developmental pattern known as the *family life cycle*. These can be thought of as the expectable events that most families go through in a fairly standard sequence. Other stresses can be thought of as traumatic or unexpectable, in that they are extraordinary; they are not necessarily experienced by most families or they occur outside of the normal sequence. Thus, each family finds its own balance between those forces tending to keep it stable and those encouraging change.

THE FAMILY LIFE CYCLE

The longitudinal view of the family's development has been referred to as its "life cycle" (Fig. 1), like the individual life cycle. As in individual development, the family evolves through expectable phases. These expectable phases include, among others, the well-known ones, such as engagement, marriage, and honeymoon; birth of the first child; first child going off to school; adolescence of the offspring; offspring's marriage and separation from home; one spouse's retirement; death of a spouse; and so forth.

In addition there are the traumatic or unexpected stresses on the family. Sometimes these consist of one of the normal phases coming out of turn, such as the unexpected death of a spouse or parent at an early age. Other stresses are the illness or incapacitation of a family member, financial reverses, and the like. In general, these traumatic changes have to do with someone entering or leaving the sphere of the family, either actually or imminently, a threatened or actual role change (for example, job change or loss) for a family member, or such a change being, for some reason, markedly delayed or distorted. The family's longitudinal course with specific developmental phases necessitates that prior stages have been more or less successfully mastered. There are various phase-specific psychosocial tasks which need to be worked out at each stage and the extent to which these phases have been successfully mastered will depend to a considerable degree on the flexibility and functionality of the family as a whole and of its component parts.[5]

A good deal of work has been done in studying and elucidating phase-specific tasks for each of these years in family life. Here, as an example, we will discuss briefly the tasks involved in the earliest stages of Phase I, Beginning Family, consisting of the engagement, marriage, and honeymoon. (This discussion is based on the work of Rhona Rapoport[6,7] and that of Evelyn M. Duvall.[8])

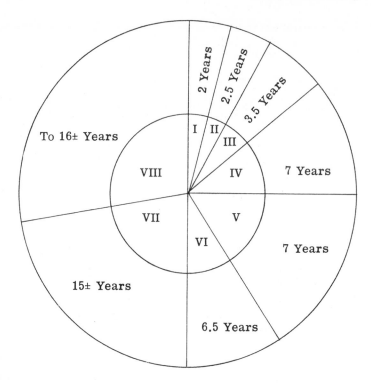

Phase	Family phase	Family description
I	Beginning family	Married couple without children
II	Childbearing family	Oldest child, up to 30 months
III	Families of preschool children	Oldest child, 30 months to 6 years
IV	Families with school children	Oldest child, 6-13 years
V	Families with teenagers	Oldest child, 13-20 years
VI	Families as launching centers	First child gone to last child leaving home
VII	Families in the middle years	Empty nest to retirement
VIII	Aging families	Retirement to death of both spouses

Fig. 1.   The Family Life Cycle[8]

Engagement phase.   Rapoport stated:

The three tasks considered by us to be salient in this area of *intrapersonal* preparation for marriage are: (I) making oneself ready to take over the role of husband/wife; (II) disengaging (or altering the form of engagement) of oneself from especially close relationships that *compete* or interfere with commitment to the new marital relationship; (III) accommodating patterns of gratifications of premarital life to patterns of the newly formed couple (marital) relationship (p. 74).[6]

And, further on:

This leads to consideration of the second major group of engagement tasks, namely those involved in the couple's *interpersonal* preparation for marriage. . . .
The tasks we have specified in this area are:
1. establishing a couple identity;
2. developing a mutually satisfactory sexual adjustment for the engagement period;
3. developing a mutually satisfactory system of communication between the pair;
4. establishing a mutually satisfactory pattern with regard to relatives;
5. developing a mutually satisfactory pattern with regard to friends;
6. developing a mutually satisfactory pattern with regard to work;
7. developing mutually satisfactory patterns of decision making;
8. planning specifically for the wedding, honeymoon, and the early months of marriage that lie ahead (pp. 76–77).[6]

Honeymoon phase. In the honeymoon phase, the work seems to involve the following:

Intrapersonal Task I: Developing a competence to pariticipate in an appropriate sexual relationship with one's marital partner . . . . *Intrapersonal Task II:* Developing competence to live in close association with the marital partner . . . . *Interpersonal Task I:* Developing the basis for a mutually satisfactory sexual relationship . . . . *Interpersonal Task II:* Having a mutually satisfactory shared experience as a basis for developing a later husband-wife relationship (pp. 44–46).[8]

Individual marital systems can be evaluated in terms of the processes by which they have attempted to deal with their appropriate tasks, and the outcome of these attempts.

FAMILY TASKS[5]

Provision of Basic Physical Needs: Food, Shelter, Clothing

The essential life-maintaining tasks of the family group may at times be overlooked by middle-class therapists treating middle-class families. Those who have come into contact with family systems in which these basics have not been provided, become much more aware that there is a fundamental biological requirement for families. To the extent that these needs are not adequately met, or are dealt with in idiosyncratic fashion, all the more complex functions of the family will in one way or another be affected so as to be distorted or deficient. A therapist must pay attention to the basic "reality factors" and, where indicated, the major, or at least the initial effort, may have to be to help the family deal more adequately with its basic needs. A family system already overwhelmed by gross deficiencies in basic needs will not usually be motivated or sensitive to more sophisticated or symbolic considerations.

Special techniques have been devised for helping lower class families, ghetto families, and highly disorganized families. The work of Minuchin[9] and others[10,11] indicates that it is both necessary and possible to help these families deal with some of the basic needs by using indigenous populations as family advocates with social agencies, by mobilizing the most constructive forces in the family system, and by providing training in basic task performance.

Development of a Marital Coalition

The core of the family is the marital coalition. This term implies that the spouses have been able to loosen their ties appropriately from their families of origin and have been able to develop a sense of their own individuality and self-worth.

Haley[12] has pointed out that marriage is not only a joining together of two individuals, but also a distillation of their families of origin, each with its own experiences, history, life style, and attitudes. One marries not only an individual, but also the family context in which the individual lives. In addition, actual members of these original families often play important roles in the new family (for example, "in-law" problems).

Extended families influence the nuclear family. If grandparents are alive, they may be involved very clearly and specifically in the daily operations of nuclear families (they may take sides, comment on child-rearing practices, live next door). But even when the extended family is not physically present, the patterns experienced by the spouses in their original families inevitably will influence their current marital and family interaction. The "three generation hypothesis"[13,14] refers to the notion that behavior may be passed down from generation to generation as projection can be passed on as a primary defense mechanism from father to son to grandson. In doing therapy, therefore, one must constantly bear in mind the "presence" of these "third parties."[15]

The couple must be able to work together toward common goals and to establish both complementary and symmetrical relationships that are functional and satisfactory to them. A *complementary relationship* occurs when two people exchange different sorts of behavior (for example, giving and receiving). A *symmetrical relationship* occurs when two people exchange the same behavior (for example, both partners giving). When a couple is unable to form either of these relationships, the marriage to that extent may be restricted.[12]

Haley further pointed out that the process of working out a satisfactory marital relationship can be seen as a process of working out shared agreements, largely undiscussed, between the two people involved. These agreements may consist of explicit rules, implied rules, which the couple would agree to if they were pointed out to them, and rules that an observer would note, but that the couple itself probably would deny. Seen this way, conflict in marriage is brought about when there are disagreements about the rules of living together, disagreements about who is to set those rules, and attempts to enforce rules that are mutually incompatible. For example, there may be disagreements as to whether the husband or the wife should wash the dishes, but there may be further disagreement as to who should make this decision. More complex still is the situation in which one spouse forces the other to agree "voluntarily" to wash the dishes.

The extent to which these issues involving family rules, roles, and coalitions are satisfactorily clarified and developed, and the manner in which the process occurs, are related to the couple's style of communicating thoughts, feelings, and attitudes. Partners who are experienced in expressing themselves and are "permitted" to do so about relevant, meaningful interpersonal issues will stand a better chance of coping competently with the challenges of family living. To the degree that the marriage is one in which members are not "free" or accustomed to indicating their concerns and needs, the marriage will be hampered in dealing productively with the inevitable stresses that befall it. Each of these two styles may be self-reinforcing, so that "virtuous" and "vicious" cycles, respectively, may be set up.

The functions of marriage for the spouses will involve an opportunity for them to deal with their sexual needs and may offer, in part, a relationship of friends in which there is mutual sharing of feelings, interests, activities, availability, and emotional support. Historically, marriages were based to a large extent on economic considerations; this continues to be the case today, but at times is not so prominent. Marriage offers a fairly practical and acceptable way to conceive and raise children. Marriage seems to offer a sense of stability, continuity, and meaningful direction into the future. For some, marriage is a response to a variety of social pressures that sanction and reinforce it as an institution. For any two individuals, marriage may afford the opportunity for the meshing of particular psychological traits and needs.

The marital coalition over the entire course of the family life cycle is marked by changing circumstances. Usually, the spouses have a period of time alone together as husband and wife before the arrival of offspring. Later, they must accommodate to being a father or mother and also part of a *parental dyad,* in addition to being either husband or wife as part of a *marital dyad.* With the passage of time, the parental role decreases in functional significance and the marital partnership becomes the primary, perhaps almost the exclusive, dyad once again.

Of course, to the extent that the marital interaction has atrophied while the children were being parented, there will be difficulty in letting go of the children. A major readjustment will be necessary when the two partners find themselves alone together in an empty house after the children have grown, having to take up again the roles of husband and wife. Figure 1 makes clear that the average family unit will find the marital partners alone together for about half the total family life after children have left home. For about half of this period the breadwinner often is no longer working (thereby losing another important role function and self-esteem support) and the two marital partners are together much more than in the previous years.

Personality Development and Enculturation of Offspring

UTILIZATION OF AGE-APPROPRIATE CHILD-REARING TECHNIQUES

Both parents should have at their disposal the techniques for child rearing and the emotional capacity for relating appropriately to the offspring at each phase of development.

Each stage provides opportunities as well as pitfalls. The decision to have a child; the period of pregnancy, birth, and the immediate neonatal period; the varying and insistent demands of the infant and the growing child, and then of school years, adolescence, and further independence, culminating in the offspring leaving home and forming their own families; and then relating to offspring as co-adults—these constitute a process that is amazingly complex and challenging. It is not surprising that families experience many difficulties along the way. For many individuals, parenthood will be one of the most fulfilling roles in their lives, but for others it will seem painful and unrewarding. Marital partners may be relatively unsophisticated and ignorant with respect to appropriate techniques and cultural expectations relating to various developmental phases. They may have particular difficulty in some specific phase, perhaps related to what they experienced in their own families of origin. They may find it difficult to move from one stage to another, and may find themselves "hanging on" inappropriately to a stage that is past. For example, some families seem to be particularly invested in and do a good job with infants and children, but the adolescence of their offspring is a stormy, troublesome time.

Mr. and Mrs. Z. can serve as an illustration. In their late thirties, they had a great deal of experience in raising puppies and raising violets, and only after a considerable period of marriage had decided to have a child. Since the birth of their child, there had been an increasing amount of fighting and this interfered with their functioning. They had done quite well when their son was an infant, enjoying diapering, feeding, and so forth, but as soon as he became autonomous and had desires of his own, they found that he upset the routine they had worked out over many years. For example, he would upset their flower pots and did not want to eat at regular mealtimes that had been set for the past 13 years. Suddenly and inexplicably, they found themselves fighting about limits.

Families may become so rigid that they are unable to move successfully into the next phase. For example, it is the job of the family, among other things, to make sure that during late adolescence the children are appropriately emancipated from the family. This will be a difficult task for families in which the spouses do not have a gratifying marital relationship to fill the void created when the children are away from the family. Such parents may refuse to let the adolescents out of the house to date or otherwise spend time with their age-peers.

MAINTENANCE OF THE PARENTAL COALITION

Assured roles in the marital coalition referred to above will broaden to include the marital partners' attitudes as *parents* toward child-rearing attitudes and practices. It is beneficial to have parental agreement and consistency in these areas, with a sharing of responsibility and mutual support. A child becomes confused if he does not know what is expected of him, or if he receives continually conflicting messages from each of his parents. Clearly, parents cannot agree on everything, and there may be danger in attempting to present a facade of agreement that is in fact only pseudoagreement, However, on basic important matters, it is preferable to have some sort of stable parental guidelines rather than parents who are unable to agree on anything.

Mr. and Mrs. L. were only-children who married in their late twenties. They both had been favorite children of their respective extended families. They found in the early years of their marriage that whenever a decision had to be made (as it did some 30 or 40 times a day), decision making was accomplished by one partner "winning" and the other "losing." When they had children, this pattern continued and was accentuated by the children's own desires. The children quickly found that they could get what they wanted by aligning themselves with one parent or the other. The couple sought treatment at the point where they were unable to communicate and agree about anything, because discussion exploded into throwing of pots and pans, with the children "cheering them on."

Why are two parents required? The parent of the same sex as an offspring serves as a role model for identification, while the parent of the opposite sex provides the basic love object and, thus, the sense of self-worth. In a family in which the parents do not form a workable coalition, the child has difficulty with these mechanisms. In a family in which one parent is absent (through death or divorce, for example), at certain critical periods in the child's development personality defects of various types may be formed unless the remaining parent or a parent surrogate is able to fill the role of the absent parent.[16]

A critical factor, when one parent is absent, seems to be the quality of the parental relationship prior to the loss of the parent. If the parents got along well, then the loss of one of them may be much less significant for the child than if they did not get along well. The remaining spouse is able to encourage positive rather than negative identification with the lost parent. The relationship that existed between the lost parent and the child is also of crucial importance to adjustment following "parental deprivation." If parent and child got along well before the separation, then there is a much greater likelihood of the child's continuing to do well after the separation. In one case, a father of a seven-year-old son often took him fishing, put him to bed every evening, and participated in most other child-rearing decisions. After the loss of his father, the son showed no decline in functioning.

Parents may be able to maintain a reasonable coalition with respect to their children and be relatively good parents, even though in other areas there may be considerable marital disharmony. This is sometimes seen in the extreme case in which the spouses have been divorced but are able to maintain good parental functioning. In some families, the opposite can be seen. The marital relationship functions fairly adequately, but the two spouses seem unwilling or unable to devote the requisite amount of time, energy, and interest to the parental role, so they are good marital partners, but relatively poor parents. This is sometimes the case with immature, selfish, or narcissistic parents.

In the families of patients viewed as "seriously disturbed," the parents may, instead of forming a workable coalition, (1) deprecate each other in a hostile manner, (2) become rivals for the child, (3) equate loyalty to the other parent with rejection of themselves, (4) indicate that growing up to be like the other parent is unacceptable, or (5) promote unhealthy parent-child dyads. The child may respond by (1) trying to bridge the gap between parents, (2) feeling or being held responsible for the parents' problems (the scapegoat role), or (3) supporting or completing the life of that parent the child feels he needs to cater to the most.

Often, the child considered disturbed is the bond that holds the marriage together, the parents in many ways being dependent upon the child's problems to keep the focus off their own relationship. Improvement in the child may then be expected to cause disruption in the parental relationship.

MAINTENANCE OF GENERATION BOUNDARIES

Broadly speaking, parents must act like parents and children like children. Of course, the nature of the generation boundary changes at various stages of the family life cycle. Thus, the nurturing role of parents in relation to their children is different when the child is 1 week old and when he is 40 years old. Parents should not be emotionally dependent upon their immature children but, rather, should look to one another for support and reinforcement.

The R. family consisted of father, mother, older daughter, and two sons. Mr. R. was barely able to hold a half-time job, while Mrs. R. stayed at home, alternately complaining of various bodily ailments and crying hysterically. In this family, the daughter planned and cooked the meals, the two sons both worked to supplement the family income, and the three children together did the planning of family activities each week. When major decisions had to be made, the older son would call the family together; the parents would be brought into the room and would then sit almost quietly by while the three children made the decision, such as how to finance a family house. Although this may seem incredible and somewhat farfetched, the authors have seen many such cases.

In the B. family, the father had been killed in an automobile accident soon after the third daughter was born. Mrs. B. found herself overwhelmed by having to raise her three daughters, and had turned over the job to the oldest daughter. This daughter had become overly rigid in enforcing limits, not allowing either of her two younger sisters to date, and the two younger sisters were at war with her. The eldest sister at age 19 felt deprived of her own chance to "have fun."

The maintenance of generation boundaries tends to lessen role conflicts that follow upon the blurring of roles and the ambiguity this fosters. A totally "democratic" family in which all members, regardless of age, responsibility, experience, and so forth, have an equal voice in all decisions seems to us wholly unrealistic. A "generation gap" between parents and children, far from being something to be decried, is an absolute necessity, if we mean by the term a difference in responsibility, role, maturity, and often of attitude. It should not, however, consist of a deficiency in communication. Recognition must be given to the different affectional relationships that of necessity exist between the parents and between parent and child. Emotional room must be left for the child to invest in learning, peer group activities, and the child's own identity.

In a seriously disturbed family, parents may exist in a childlike dependency on one another, they may be rivals for the child's affection or may be jealous of the child; incestuous tendencies may become marked and may be acted upon, and parents may leave decision making to the child, rather than appropriately assume that responsibility themselves.[17]

To the extent that parents are dissatisfied with their own lives, they may tend to compete with their offspring and be jealous of them. In the movie of several years back, *The Graduate,* there was a blatant example of a suburban mother who, unhappy in her marriage and troubled about her approaching middle age, became an active romantic rival for her daughter's boyfriend.

In those families in which parents feel inadequate in their parental role, perhaps because of unfortunate experiences in their own family of origin, they may tend to be inappropriately and unrealistically permissive and abdicate many of the duties and responsibilities that revolve around the role of parent. In other instances, because of economic or other realistic pressures, an older child may be called upon to fulfill a parental role with the younger sibs, and may sustain a type of personality warping by not having had the opportunity to experience and master the developmental tasks of childhood or adolescence.

The overly dictatorial parent at least offers his offspring a clear model (if only one to revolt against), although he often may be using the child to attempt to master some unresolved issues in himself. Often such parents find it extremely difficult to "let go," and to realize that after a certain stage, offspring have become autonomous. The parents have done the best they could and need no longer feel responsibility for their children, but rather should deal with them as fellow adults.

Special problems exist in this regard in a society such as our own, which is extremely youth-oriented and in which the rate of change is constantly accelerating. In such a society, it is hard for parents and children to feel that what the parents have to offer is "relevant." Children are bombarded by outside influences from the communications media (notably T.V.). The age-peer group may prematurely come to be a dominating influence. Parents (and their children) may become confused, and as a consequence some may throw up their hands in permissiveness, while others put their foot down in authoritarianism.

ADHERENCE TO APPROPRIATE SEX-LINKED ROLES

The sexual identity of the offspring is an important factor in personality formation. Appropriate sex-linked role attributes develop not merely by the accident of biologically male or female birth, but are acquired by role allocations starting in infancy, together with role assumptions and identifications as the child grows older. The crucial factor in determining one's basic sexual identity (that is, whether one regards oneself as basically a male or a female) is how we are dealt with in this respect by our parents. This factor will be dominant even if it contradicts every known biological gender indicator. Even clearer are the environmental influences in gender-role (how masculine or feminine we consider ourselves to be, and what the components of this identity are).

Lidz[5] has considered that clear-cut role reversals with respect to sexual functioning and task divisions lead to important distortions in the child's development. This traditional view holds that the female should be the expressive-affectional gender and the male should be the instrumental-adaptive gender. Furthermore, a cold, affectionless mother would be relatively more harmful to the offspring, and especially to female offspring, than would a cold, affectionless father. A weak, ineffective father, on the other hand, would tend to be more damaging to the offspring, especially the male offspring, than would a weak, ineffective mother.

These traditional, idealized gender roles have been increasingly challenged in recent years, viz., recent changes in sex-appropriate grooming and dress, the emergence of changing attitudes in women, and so forth. Underlying this may be our emergence into an era in which an increasing number of individuals will be more free to explore whatever potentialities exist within themselves, without being constrained by gender stereotypes imposed by society. The negative aspect of this development lies in the fostering of greater sexual and gender confusion.

The S. family consisted of father, mother, and two children, aged 9 and 7. The father had been raised in a "female dominated" family consisting of his mother, his aunt, and his four sisters. In this marriage, he did the housework and cooking and felt "I'm not up to working." The mother worked in a steel mill and was known to "swear like a longshoreman." She dressed in a masculine way and managed the family finances. The son and daughter complained in the course of therapy that their identity was "confused."

Rossi[18] has reviewed the changing roles of women in the family over the past 50 years. She finds that women now devote a smaller percentage of their adult life to the rearing of children. They have achieved higher levels of education, facilitating more egalitarian relations between husbands and wives.

ENCULTURATION OF THE OFFSPRING

It is one of the tasks of parents to teach the younger generation the basic adaptive techniques of the culture. It is necessary for them to transmit instrumentally valid ways of thinking, feeling, and acting.

Communication skills are basic for any type of successful and gratifying social interaction and personality growth. Parents usually play the major role in the proper development of these skills by their children. They themselves will be models for the children, in behavior and in the appropriate and effective methods of expressing thoughts and feelings. Children need to be given the proper labels and comments with respect to what and how they feel and think. A child who is clearly angry needs to have this feeling recognized and labeled for him, rather than having a parent consistently deny, overlook, or misinterpret his feelings. He needs to be given permission to experience his own feelings as valid, and not be restricted to those his parents would find more convenient.

It has been shown that we learn basic rules of how and what to think, feel, and do, primarily as a result of early family experiences. What thoughts, feelings, and actions are acceptable, how and under what circumstances they may be expressed, as well as general styles of interacting and fundamental attitudes toward ourselves and the environment—all this is laid down in our early and repeated transactions with our parents.

In pathological families, various difficulties in these areas may be noted. Members of dysfunctional families may show particularly intrusive, projective, tangential, concretistic, or bizarre thinking. There may be considerable ambiguity and vagueness, and a prevailing feeling of meaninglessness. Some investigators have especially noted these difficulties in families of schizophrenic patients (see Chapter 11).

A child's emotions may be distorted in some families in a major way by being fairly consistently denied, contradicted, ignored, erroneously explained, or punished. For example, in some families sadness or disappointment cannot be expressed because it makes the parents "upset."

Certain families seem to have difficulty teaching their children socially acceptable techniques of behavior, and these children seem to grow up with either a deficient or a distorted repertory of social-behavioral skills. Both overly authoritarian and overly permissive attitudes in the parents may lead to inflexible, maladaptive patterns in the children.

REFERENCES

1. Family life in America (editorial). N Engl J Med 274:1209, 1966.
2. Birdwhistell R: The idealized model of the American family. Social Casework 51:195–198, 1970.
3. Ackerman N: Family therapy, in Arieti S (ed): American Handbook of Psychiatry, vol III. New York, Basic Books, 1966, pp 201–212.
4. American Psychiatric Association. A Psychiatric Glossary. New York, The Association, 1967.
5. Lidz T: The Family and Human Adaptation. New York, International Universities Press, 1963.
6. Rapoport R: Normal crises, family structure and mental health. Family Process 2:68–80, 1963.
7. Rapoport R, Rapoport R N: New light on the honeymoon. Human Relations, 17:33–56, 1964
8. Duvall E: Family Development. Philadelphia, Lippincott, 1967.
9. Minuchin S, Montalvo B, Guerney B G, Rosman B L, and Shumer F: Families of the Slums: An Exploration of Their Structure and Treatment. New York, Basic Books, 1967.
10. Sager C, Brayboy T, Waxenberg B: Black Ghetto Family in Therapy: A Laboratory Experience. New York, Grove Press, 1970.
11. McKinney J: Adapting family therapy to multi-deficit families. Social Casework 51:327–333, 1970.
12. Haley J: Marriage therapy. Arch Gen Psychiatry 8:213–234, 1963.
13. Mendell D, Cleveland S: A three-generation view of a school phobia. Voices 3:16–19, 1967.
14. Mendell D, Cleveland S, Fisher S: A five-generation family theme. Family Process 7:126–132, 1968.
15. Zuk G: Triadic-based family therapy. Int J Psychiatry 8:539–569, 1969.
16. Block J: Lives Through Time. Berkeley, California, Bancroft, 1971.
17. Coe W C, Curry A E, Kessler D R: Family interactions of psychiatric patients. Family Process 8:119–130, 1969.
18. Rossi A: Family development in a changing world. Am J Psychiatry 128:1057–1066, 1972.

3

Understanding the
Dysfunctional Family

OBJECTIVES

- To understand how disturbances in the family system, family life cycle, family tasks and myths, are thought to produce dysfunctional families
- To appreciate how disturbances in families develop in terms of the relationship of "symptoms" and family homeostasis
- To understand the theories of how one individual comes to be the identified patient

We have been attempting to understand the structure and function of the family. The concept of the family as a system, the family life cycle, the notion of family tasks, and the relation of these to family disturbances have been discussed. In this chapter, the discussion will be extended and case examples will be presented.

THE DYSFUNCTIONAL FAMILY SYSTEM

Members of dysfunctional families appear to lack a healthy sense of involvement and interaction in a developing and differentiating group. In many such families, members have the most tentative, minimal contact with each other. They may be physically separated from one another in a variety of ways and for a variety of reasons. They may rarely speak with one another,[1-3] or their topics of conversation may rarely deal with important family issues. Their emotional involvement with one another may be flimsy, and instead of feeling close to one another, they may be rather cold and distant. Such families are likely to develop a sense of noncohesiveness, pervading meaninglessness, and noncommitment.[4,5]

> The father in the M. family was a 40-year-old Baptist. The mother was a 25-year-old Methodist. In their section of the country, such religious differences were marked. The father worked on the night shift as a factory worker, the mother worked as a secretary. They saw each other for about 5 minutes in the morning before she went to work and 5 minutes at night before he went to work. They came into treatment as they began to be more and more suspicious of each other, coincident to the gradually decreasing communication that had evolved over a period of 2 years.

At the other extreme are those families in which there appears to be little or no differentiation of members, but rather a relatively nonindividualized mass.[4] Members appear to be cohesive, but are more accurately described as agglutinated. There is a pseudocloseness not based on individual needs, feelings, and stages. Under the surface, the same weaknesses may emerge in this type of family as in the type with minimal contact.

Families with such defects will have serious problems in coping with the challenges and developments of family life. Families whose members cannot satisfactorily communicate with each other and who have not defined themselves as individuals suffer from basic defects. Such failures in being able to respond satisfactorily lead to further deterioration of already gravely inadequate basic problem-solving capacities.

> The R. family consisted of the father, who was in his late forties, the mother, who was in her early forties, and the son, Sam, in his early twenties. Sam was the identified patient, having schizophrenia. Though seemingly close as a family, in fact the mother and father had long since given up sexual relations or even attending social functions together. Sam had dropped out of school and was staying in the house talking to his guitar and watching television. The mother was barely able to keep up with the housework, saying that she eventually intended to clean up her closet and was studying how to do gardening. Close inspection revealed that the father was barely able to do his job, managing by simply following the same routine as a salesman as he had done for years and years. He was barely eking out a living. They never seemed to disagree with one another on anything. Individual members were not able to allocate time on an individual basis, but did everything "together." They were afraid to deal with differ-

entness. There was a pervading sense of emptiness—the mother spent much of her time in bed, the father complained of not getting any satisfaction from work or his family, and the son felt "hopeless."

THE LIFE CYCLE OF THE DYSFUNCTIONAL FAMILY

While some families will be plagued by major generalized problems throughout the family's existence, others will have trouble at specific periods. More episodic family difficulties may be related to an inability to cope adequately with the tasks of the current family phase, the need to move on to a new family phase, and the stress of traumatic, excessive, and out-of-order events in the family developmental cycle.

The stresses and difficulties may be those attendant on the normal, expectable family life crises. The marriage or family may be unable to cope adequately with the current phase in its life cycle, and any particular phase of the family cycle may be affected, depending on a variety of factors relating to the adequacy and availability of the family members' resources for accomplishing the tasks inherent in their current stage.

For example, as indicated in Chapter 2, two individuals optimally need to have reached a certain stage in their own personal development, including their relationships with their own families of origin, before being ready, as two independent individuals, to consider getting married. To the extent that this and other, prior, stages have not been successfully mastered, the individuals and the marital unit will be hampered in dealing with current challenges. This concept obviously applies to each of the family phases.

Everyone is familiar with the young married couple who cannot break away from their own families to establish a successful marriage.

On their wedding night, Mr. and Mrs. W. found they were unable to have intercourse because of Mrs. W.'s nausea and vomiting. Mr. W. became so depressed the couple had to return from the honeymoon after one night. Soon after this, both husband and wife found themselves spending so much time with their own parents, after work, that they had very little time for each other, and "sex just never seemed to get off the ground." Each partner developed a feeling of anger and resentment toward the other and their communication became markedly decreased. At the same time, their social life became more restricted and they were unable to plan any events together. They came to therapy at the point where they were considering divorce.

Another typical family problem is the "shotgun marriage." Here, two people become instant marital partners and parents, and on an involuntary basis, at that. In this process, various developmental phases are skipped altogether or are frantically condensed, for example, individuation, engagement, marriage, honeymoon, marital union.

Mrs. V. came for treatment following a suicide attempt. Her father was a chronic alcoholic; her mother was a hardworking, conscientious secretary. She had married a boy she had known for 4 months, after discovering that she was pregnant. Although she "didn't really care for him" she married in order not to "disgrace the family." Following the marriage there was instantaneous cessation of sex and screaming fights, which culminated in her suicide attempt.

In other cases, families may find it extremely stressful or impossible to move into the next appropriate phase. Marriages and families may have been in chronic difficulty, having attempted for some time to deal with the requirements of a particular phase. Or, they may have appeared to cope quite successfully until the transition into a new phase of the family cycle plunged them into distress and dysfunction. Change is difficult, and the need to modify or abandon old familiar roles and patterns of interaction and take on new "strange" ways is not easy. The "empty nest syndrome" is one such phase.

The J. family had four teenage children, the youngest of whom was 16, and the oldest 20. All the children lived with their parents and were forbidden to date. On the occasional times when the family did go out, they went out as a family to "noncontroversial" movies. The family was referred by the juvenile court after the oldest child had run away several times. Inquiry revealed that both parents, although insisting that they wanted their children to grow up, to get to be on their own, were quite frightened about being alone in the house with just each other. They described such a possibility as frightening and at times had a fear that it would be unsatisfactory.

To some extent, every family has difficulty in mastering expected phases of the family cycle and unexpected life changes, and this is even truer for the more disturbed families. However, it may be of some help to keep these two areas separate, as the marital or family therapist evaluates the particular family unit he is seeing.

Thus far, only the usual expectable sequence of family developmental phases has been discussed. However, even more difficulty may be experienced when traumatic, excessive, and out-of-order changes in the family life cycle take place. Unusual, unexpected events in the family life cycle may overwhelm the coping capacities of family systems that might otherwise have been relatively well able to handle developmental changes, had they occurred expectably, in the usual sequence, and over an extended period of time.

The Q. family consisted of the father, an engineer; the mother, a housewife; and an infant daughter, age 3. The father suddenly was drafted into the Army. At this point, the mother, who had always been extremely close to her own parents, felt lost and abandoned. She found great difficulty in taking care of the house and her daughter. The daughter was the identified patient, referred by the pediatrician because of "setting fires." Further examination of the situation revealed that the mother was so depressed that she would go to bed early, leaving the daughter to play on her own for a couple of hours. During this time, the daughter managed to climb up to the stove and light a piece of paper that could be used to light other pieces of paper. The father was brought home to be with his family. The mother got out of bed and the fire setting stopped.

The phase of the family life cycle may help to explain the timing of the marital or family disturbance. Other factors are related to inability to accomplish family tasks, to dysfunctional family myths, to the type of disturbance manifested by the family system, and the particular family member manifesting the disturbance.

TASKS IN THE DYSFUNCTIONAL FAMILY

Various deficiencies in carrying out the family's functions will lead to strains and distortions in family life. The major family tasks, as discussed earlier, are

1. To provide for the basic physical requirements
2. To develop a working marital coalition capable of dealing with the stages of the family life cycle
3. To rear the offspring

Under these headings in Chapter 2 are detailed the kinds of situations that may arise when these tasks are not fulfilled.

FAMILY MYTHS

Individuals and families have systems of belief that determine their feelings and behavior. These attitudes, largely unexpressed directly, run below the surface of the family's interactions, and help to shape its general outline and its specific features. These subterranean structures have been referred to as "family myths." They are often found to be important roots of family difficulty, and the family therapist must be aware of them if he is to understand family behavior that might otherwise seem inexplicable.

In discussing below some of the important and frequent myths that seem to cause difficulty, we have attempted to include those that seem most prominent in the experience of family therapists.[6-8] It is not to be expected that everyone will agree with the value judgments about these myths that are expressed here. Rather, each therapist must work out for himself his own values with respect to these issues (It should be kept in mind that it is literally impossible not to have values and not to convey them to families being treated.). The therapist must be sensitive to and deal appropriately with those attitudes and beliefs that seem to be deleterious to a family's functioning.

Marriage and family should be totally happy, and each individual therein should of necessity expect either all or a major part of his gratifications to come from the family system. This romantic myth dies hard in some quarters. The idea that many of life's satisfactions are to be found outside the family setting must be made clear, indicating that there is a whole range of gratifying patterns that families work out to fit their own particular components.

The "togetherness" myth. To what extent will merely remaining in close physical proximity or carrying out all activities jointly lead to satisfactory family life and individual gratification? Again, there will probably be great variation from one family to another, but surely this cannot be held up as an ideal pattern for all families under all conditions.

Marital partners should be totally honest with one another at all times. In its modern guise, much of this idea may be derived from experience with "encounter groups" in which people are encouraged to express their feelings freely (especially negative ones, it seems), and also from the concept that what is held back or repressed will of necessity do us harm eventually in one way or another. There is, however, little evidence to indicate this, and in fact full and open frankness in feeling, action, and thought may cause at least as much harm as good. Experience has also shown that "honesty" can be enlisted in the service of hostility as much as in the service of a constructive, problem-solving approach. Many people feel that a degree of interpersonal sensitivity will often mitigate against this concept of "total honesty," and that many hurtful statements, especially regarding factors that cannot be changed, are perhaps best left unspoken.

A happy marriage is one in which there are no disagreements, and when family members fight with one another it means that they hate each other. It seems inevitable that family members will have differences with one another and that these will often lead to overt disagreements.

These, in turn, may lead to "fights" or arguments, but if these are constructive and nonpersonal, clarification and potential solution can be found without anyone suffering loss of esteem. However, many families seem afraid to disagree and cover up differences by pseudoagreement. On the other hand, there are families that fight all the time about almost every issue, but seemingly are not able to resolve any disagreements; instead, they seem to resort to personal attacks on each other's motives, veracity, and the like.

The marital partners should see eye-to-eye on every issue and should work toward being as identical in outlook as possible. It seems to us that the first part of this statement is just about impossible, and the second part is of questionable benefit. Here again, open recognition of the inevitable differences of the marital partners may be a helpful first step, as may also be the recognition of the gains to the individual, as well as to the family unit, from differences that can be used constructively. It is remarkable how often we see married couples who seem either unwilling to recognize or incapable of recognizing the inevitable differences between the two partners with respect to past experience, basic attitudes, personality styles, and the like. Instead, there often seems to be a marked projection of one's personality attributes, both positive and negative, onto the partner, with relatively little ability to see the partner more realistically as he or she actually is.

Marital partners should be as unselfish as possible and give up thinking about their own individual needs. Clearly, it is possible to go too far in the opposite direction as well, and most successful marriages seem to operate somewhere in the mid-range in this respect. But we certainly have seen marriages in which an individual has unsuccessfully tried to pretend that he or she was not an individual with particular needs and satisfactions, but rather merely a satellite or undifferentiated mass attached to some larger family system, for example, mother lives only for the sake of the family. We think it is quite possible and often necessary for successful family units to recognize the differential allocations and satisfactions to be derived from one's role as an individual human being, as a marital partner, as a parent, and so forth.

When something goes wrong in the family, one should look around to see who is at fault. Most of us have been overtrained in this manner of thinking, so that we almost reflexively think in terms of either our own guilt or someone else's, at times of dissatisfaction. Customary and useful as this may be at times, in many instances it tends to be self-defeating and even semi-autonomous. That is to say, there seems to be a certain perverse satisfaction or benefit to be derived merely from the ability to assess and assign blame. An alternative viewpoint that is often useful, especially in nongratifying family interactions, is that when things go wrong, it is in relation to the interactional properties of the entire system, and these must be looked at with a problem-solving approach, in a relatively nonpersonalized, nonblaming manner. This may lead more satisfactorily to appropriate and gratifying solutions. In other types of family situations, a preliminary step, where there seems to be excessive emphasis on blaming, is to encourage each family member to ask himself or herself what has been his part or role in what has been going on, and what could each then do individually to produce a more gratifying result. We have sometimes used the analogy of two pieces of a jigsaw puzzle that do not seem to fit well together. In such an instance which of the two pieces of the puzzle is to blame?

When things are not going well, it will often be of help to spend a major part of the time digging up past as well as present hurts. Arguments that involve seemingly endless recriminations about past disappointments and difficulties may serve to give temporary relief by allowing the parties to ventilate, but this often leads only to futile escalation of the argument, with a sort of "Can you top this?" discussion. Besides usually making things worse rather than better, this actively detracts from any constructive attempts at problem solving by taking up considerable amounts of time and emotional energy. Often one of the first jobs of the family therapist is to act as a kind of "traffic cop" in stopping these nonproductive family maneuvers. It should be kept in mind that nothing can be done to change what has happened in the past, and that "crying over spilt milk" rarely in and of itself does much good unless it leads, for example, to increased understanding of present patterns and to some attempts at modifying those that are unsatisfactory.

In a marital argument one partner is right and the other is wrong, and the goal of such fights should be for the partners to see which one can score the most "points." Obviously, the contrary is the case. When one marital partner wins a fight, it is usually the marriage as a whole that loses. This sort of competitiveness in the marital relationship is not usually preferred to a cooperative working together, in which neither marital partner necessarily scores points, but in which the outcome is such that both individuals and the marriage itself stand to gain.

A good sexual relationship will inevitably lead to a good marriage in general. Everyone has seen examples of individuals who married when they were physically infatuated with one another, but who woke up after the honeymoon and discovered that in respects other than physical they were relatively poorly suited to one another; at least they had many differences and situations to work out with one another that they hardly dreamed of at the time they married. Certainly, a good sexual relationship is almost invariably an important component of a satisfactory marriage, but it does not necessarily preclude the presence of difficulties in other areas.

If the marriage is satisfactory in other respects, the sexual part of it will more or less take care of itself. Certainly the recent experience of sex therapists such as Masters and Johnson[9] and other family therapists indicates that the sexual relationship may need specific attention in its own right and cannot automatically be taken for granted on the basis of a fairly functional marital relationship otherwise. Indeed, difficulties in the sexual sphere seem very commonly to lead to difficulties in the rest of the marital relationship. Specific sex therapy for the couple may be indicated, following the successful completion of which other basically secondary difficulties may evaporate.

Marital partners increasingly understand each other's nonverbal communications, so that there is little or no need to check things out with one another verbally. This statement may certainly be true for functional, nonproblem families, but it is often strikingly false for families in trouble. All too often, marital partners and other family members have made assumptions that what they have said or what they intended by nonverbal means was clearly understood by someone else, and have also assumed that they were able to read someone else's mind or facial expression or ambiguity of verbal statement. When they are encouraged in therapy specifically to check out with one another some of these assumptions, they are often shocked at their own misperceptions and misinterpretations.

Positive feedback is not as necessary in marital systems as is negative feedback. All too many marital couples seem to take for granted those aspects of their relationship that are working well and are mutually gratifying, and many appear to have gotten "out of the habit" of reflecting back to their partner when he or she has done something the other found pleasing. However, there is often less hesitancy in commenting on something that has caused hurt or disappointment. Positive reinforcement of desired behavior usually serves to increase its occurrence, and is usually a much more effective learning technique than is negative feedback or punishment.

"And then they lived happily ever after." A good marriage should *"just happen"* spontaneously, and should not need to involve any

"work" on the part of the participants. This perhaps is another carryover of the romantic idea of marriage as some type of blissful, dreamlike state, unrelated to any other type of human interaction. The sad but realistic truth, however, is that marriage involves the day-to-day and the minute-by-minute interaction of the people involved, with constant negotiation, communication, solving of problems, and so forth. Some studies have shown that dysfunctional families spend only few minutes per week talking with one another about anything meaningful related to the family interaction. It is as though it would somehow be inappropriate and "mechanical" to spend time assessing and monitoring what is happening in the marriage, whereas it is perfectly appropriate to consider carrying out such investigations in a factory. Are marital partners too inexperienced in the techniques involved, is there a whole set of negative feelings that get in the way, or have they not been encouraged and given permission to do this?

Any spouse can (and often should) be reformed and remodeled into the shape desired by the partner. In many marriages an inordinate amount of time and energy is spent in the often mutual effort to reform the spouse into the desired image. This is done commonly with little or no recognition of the fact that basic personality patterns, once fairly firmly established, are not easily modified, much less basically altered. Attempts to do so lead mainly to frustration, anger, and disillusionment. Certain characteristics may perhaps be modulated or even rechanneled, and partners can be made more sensitive to each other's reactions. But the "reform movement" marriage, while it may work satisfactorily as long as both partners consent to play the requisite roles involved, may lead to futile arguments about personal qualities, lack of cooperation, and other topics. A spouse might perhaps more profitably look at himself, assessing his own characteristics and his own awareness and sensitivity to the spouse's characteristics and reactions to him, and see in what ways he himself can improve the relationship, before making up his mind as to the ways in which his spouse needs to change.

A stable marriage is one in which things do not change and in which there are no problems. It is inconceivable to us that in any living dynamic system such a frozen situation could possibly exist functionally for any period of time. Everything we know about individuals and about families as living, changing, growing, developing systems indicates clearly that to be alive is to face continual change. Those systems that attempt to remain fixed in some unchanging mold will sooner or later find themselves out of phase with current needs and developments. On the other hand, systems have a tendency toward a dynamic equilibrium in which certain patterns and interactions repeat over time, giving a sense of continuity and stability, while at the same time the entire system is moving inevitably forward.

Everyone knows what a husband should be like and what a wife should be like. If this statement was ever true, it is certainly much less so in our present society. We are constantly bombarded with varying and, indeed, conflicting messages about what the appropriate role for husband and wife should be, and there is increasingly less agreement on this subject. This situation presents a possibility of greater confusion, but it also offers an opportunity for much greater development of each partner's and the marriage's actual potential.

If a marriage is not working properly, having children will rescue it. While the arrival of children may often temporarily make the spouses feel somewhat more worthwhile, and give them a new parental role, it has not been our experience that children are a cement that will hold poor marriages together. What often happens instead is that children become the victims of marital disharmony.

No matter how bad the marriage, it should be kept together for the sake of the children. This statement is certainly open to question, if on no other grounds than that it is not necessarily true at all that children thrive better in an unhappy marriage than they do with a relatively satisfied divorced parent. If the marriage partners stay together, the children may bear the brunt of the resentment that the partners feel for one another, with the parents feeling they have "martyred" themselves for their children's sake.

If a marriage does not work, an extramarital affair, or divorce and marriage to another spouse, will cure the situation. While on certain occasions this seems to work, often by accident, what usually seems to happen is that the new partner is uncannily similar to the rejected one, and the same nongratifying patterns begin all over again, only the names of the players having been changed.

DEVELOPMENT OF FAMILY DYSFUNCTION

Marital and family systems, like individuals, have characteristic patterns of coping with stress. In times of difficulties of the sort enumerated above, the family's first line of defense usually will be to evoke, strengthen, and emphasize characteristic adaptive patterns that the marital or family unit has used in the past. The type of disturbance resulting therefrom is similar to the rigid inflexible character defenses of an individual suffering from a personality disorder.

However, if such characteristic adaptive mechanisms are not available or fail to deal adequately with the situation, one or another family member may develop overt symptoms. The symptoms in the individual family member may be such as to cause him to be labeled as bad, sick, stupid, or crazy. The appropriate social helping institutions will become involved with that individual, and attempt to deal with his particular symptomatic expression. He then takes on the role of "the identified patient." More often than not, the family context from which the individual's symptoms emanate will be overlooked entirely, deemphasized, or inadequately attended to. The bad, sick, stupid, or crazy individual family member will be dealt with, and either will be found to be intractable or, if "improved," will soon become symptomatic again when returned to the family context or, instead, another family member may become symptomatic in some way. The underlying family disturbance will not have been dealt with.

A major tenet, therefore, of family therapy theorists is that the symptomatic family member often can usefully be thought of as indicating the more widespread disturbance in the entire family system.[10,11,12,13,14] To overlook the more general family disturbance or to deal inadequately with it means that one or another family member probably will continue to be symptomatic. The focus of understanding, evaluation, and help must be broadened to include not only the individual but also the marital and family system of which that individual is a part. It should be noted, here, that while this is an important frame of reference for family theorists, it is not the only one that may be relevant in the treatment of various types of problems (see Chapter 11).

In the X. family, Mr. and Mrs. X. found that over their 12 years of marriage their sexual relationship had become more and more unsatisfactory. They contemplated divorce. At about the same time, their son began to do poorly in school, and they sought help for this. Concurrently, they felt less concerned about the unsatisfactory nature of the marriage. As the boy's school work improved, the marital problem returned to the fore.

Dr. B. brought Mrs. B. for help because she had "headaches again." Her headaches always followed reverses in his business. Dr. B. was a hardworking but rigid person who firmly believed in "male superiority." Things had gone well for them in the early years of their marriage, until the point where Mrs. B. became dissatisfied with the role of "number two" in the marriage and pressed for equality. At that point, Dr. B. intensified the "authoritarian approach" and rather than fighting back, Mrs. B. became "depressed."

The patterns of interaction within a family cannot always be clearly related to any specific dysfunction. The reasons why a specific type of disturbance is manifested in a family system or a family member are not understood clearly at the present time, but certain tendencies and circumstances probably favor the development of one or another symptomatic expression in a particular instance.

Similarly, the reasons why one family member rather than another becomes symptomatic have not been definitively settled. A number of reasons have been described to account for this phenomenon:

1. Individual susceptibility, that is, genetic predisposition. For example, an individual who was born brain damaged and under family stress is likely to become symptomatic. Genetic temperamental differences may contribute. Chess et al.,[15] who have studied activity levels of infants, have suggested that more phlegmatic babies have a greater tendency toward developing schizophrenia, whereas more active, awake, exploring babies have a greater tendency to become delinquent.

2. The situation in the family at the time of birth. For example, a parent whose own parent died around the time of the birth of a child might use the newborn infant to work out his feelings about his own dead parent.

3. Physical illness of the child. A child who is chronically ill may have family problems projected onto him whenever he has an acute episode.

4. Precipitant in the external family. Accidents, or a death that relates somehow to one child more than another (as an eldest daughter who was with her grandmother the day she had a heart attack), may make one family member the focus for family problems.

5. Sex of a child may correspond to a particular difficulty of a parent. For example, if a father feels particularly inadequate with other males, his son may become symptomatic.

6. Birth order of siblings. The eldest child may get the major "parental loading," whereas the youngest child is often "babied" and kept dependent.

7. Family myth attached to a specific individual. Certain people in families are known as the stupid one, the smart one, the lazy one, the goodlooking one, the ugly one. First names of children and nicknames may reveal these myths. Children are sometimes named for grandparents or other people significant in the parents' past and then carry along a myth attached to that person. Girls are sometimes given names of somewhat ambiguous gender, for example, Lee, Dale, Marion, Frances, Glenette, Alberta, Carol, as though to indicate parental displeasure at having a girl. The reverse also occurs for

males. Sometimes assigned names are grossly inappropriate to the gender of the child.

The symptomatic family member may be the family scapegoat, onto whom have been displaced family difficulties, or he may be psychologically or constitutionally the weakest, the youngest, or the most sensitive family member, unable to cope in any other way with the generalized family disturbance. The identified patient may be the family member most interested or involved in the process of changing the family. An example is the teenager who wants to "save" his parents, who are not getting along. He begins to steal, gets caught, and his entire family then is referred for help.

REFERENCES

1. Rabkin R: Uncoordinated communication between marriage partners. Family Process 6:10–15, 1967.
2. Stachowiak J: Decision-making and conflict resolution in the family group, in Larson C, Dance F (eds): Perspectives on Communication. Milwaukee, Wis, University of Wisconsin, Speech Communication Center, 1968, pp 113–124.
3. Westley W, Epstein N: Patterns of intra-familial communication, in Cameron D E, Greenblatt M (eds): Recent Advances in Neuro-Physiological Research. Psychiatric Research Report No. 11. New York, American Psychiatric Association, 1959, pp 1–9.
4. Wynne L C, Ryckoff I M, Day J, Hersch S I: Pseudomutuality in the family relations of schizophrenics. Psychiatry 21:205–220, 1958.
5. Wynne L C, Singer M T: Thought disorder and family relations of schizophrenics. I. A research strategy. II. A classification of forms of thinking. Arch Gen Psychiatry 9:191–206, 1963.
6. Jackson D D, Lederer W J: Mirages of Marriage. New York, Norton, 1969.
7. Ferreira A J: Family myths and homeostasis. Arch Gen Psychiatry 9:457–463, 1963.
8. Ferreira A J: Family myths: The covert rules of the relationship. Confin Psychiatr 8:15–20, 1965.
9. Masters W, Johnson V: Human Sexual Response. Boston, Little, Brown, 1966.
10. Ackerman N W: Psychodynamics of Family Life, Diagnosis and Treatment in Family Relationships. New York, Basic Books, 1958.
11. Bell J E: Family Group Therapy. Public Health Monograph No. 64. Washington, D. C.: Department of Health, Education and Welfare, Public Health Service, 1961.
12. Carroll E J: Treatment of the family as a unit. Pennsylvania Medicine 63:57–62, 1960.

13. Bateson G, Jackson D D, Haley J, Weakland J: Towards a theory of schizophrenia. Behav Sci 1:251–264, 1956.
14. Counts R: Family crisis and the impulsive adolescent. Arch Gen Psychiatry 17:64–74, 1967.
15. Chess S, Thomas A, Birch H: Your Child Is a Person. New York, Viking, 1965.

4

Evaluating the Family

OBJECTIVES

- To enable the reader to structure his gathering of data about the family
- To formulate important problem areas in the family in preparation for planning the therapeutic approach
- To know when to use special evaluation techniques such as structured interviews, psychological testing, and home visits

Evaluation of a marital couple or family should be understood as a continuing process, begun at the first contact, but not necessarily completed at any particular point. Some initial formulation is useful to the therapist to help him marshal data and form hypotheses, but in a larger sense the evaluation is often an inextricable part of the therapy itself. As data are gathered, the therapist forms hypotheses about what is going on, based on one or another conceptual frame of reference. He attempts to assign priorities and weight to the variety of contributory variables, and sets up an overall strategy, with particular intervention tactics designed to lead to certain desired goals. (These strategies and tactics will be described in the chapters on family therapy techniques.) In this process, further data are obtained that serve to modify, confirm, or negate the original hypotheses, strategies, and tactics. These later formulations are then tested in the matrix of the family sessions, with further data being obtained, and so on.

There are several points of view regarding the type and quantity of evaluative data to be gathered. Some family therapists begin with a specific and detailed longitudinal history of the family unit and its constituent members, perhaps over three or more generations. This procedure has the advantage of permitting the family and the therapist to go over together the complex background of the present situation. The therapist will begin to understand unresolved past and present issues, and will usually gain a sense of rapport and identification with the family and its members. He may then feel more comfortable in defining problem areas and in planning strategy. The family, for its part, may benefit by reviewing together the source and evolution of its current condition, a clarifying, empathy-building process in which it has not previously engaged. The good and the bad are brought into focus, and the immediate distress is placed in a broader perspective. However, sometimes a family in crisis is too impatient to tolerate exhaustive history gathering, and in acute situations lengthy data gathering must be curtailed. (A complete and detailed outline for family history and functioning will be found in Appendix B.)

Other therapists do not appear to rely heavily on the historical approach, attempting instead to delineate the situation that brings the family for treatment at the time and to obtain a cross-sectional view of its present functioning. This procedure has the advantage of starting with what the family is most concerned about, and will not be as potentially time consuming nor as seemingly remote from the present realities as the preceding method. However, the therapist may not emerge with as sharp a focus on important family patterns, and much of the discussion may be negatively tinged because of current preoccupation by the family with its difficulty. This second approach is essentially the procedure offered in the outline below.

More experienced (and courageous) therapists may curtail past history gathering severely and may also minimize formalized discussions of the family's current situation. They may begin, instead, to deal from the outset with the family's important characteristic patterns of interaction as they are manifested in the interview setting. They may tend to utilize primarily, or exclusively, the immediate, "here and now" observable family transactions in the office, understanding these to be characteristic of the family, clarifying and commenting on them and intervening in a variety of ways. This approach has the advantage of initiating treatment right from the outset, without the delay of history-gathering procedures. There is often a heightened sense of emotional involvement, and more rapid changes may occur. However, sometimes families are frightened by such an approach, feeling threatened and defensive. Also, when specific information and patterns are allowed to emerge in this more random fashion, the therapist does not always have the same degree of certainty as to whether or not he is indeed dealing with the relevant, important family patterns. (Such a procedure is not usually recommended for beginners.)

To a considerable extent, these differences in technique may mirror differences in therapists' training, theoretical beliefs, and temperaments. Most therapists, however, probably use some combination of these approaches, as the situtation warrants. Evidence is lacking, however, to demonstrate the superiority of one style over another.

OUTLINE FOR FAMILY EVALUATION

In the belief that some practical frame of reference with respect to family evaluation will prove useful, at least to the beginning therapist, an outline is presented in Table 2. While far from exhaustive in scope, this outline does provide some anchoring points for initial understanding and planning. It is not meant to be an inflexible, unchangeable outline, and it certainly could be expanded as the situation warranted, or contracted or condensed in acute family crisis. It offers a practical alternative to gathering an exhaustive history and to plunging into the middle of the family interaction. Each of these topics will be discussed in greater detail in this chapter.

Current Phase of Family Life Cycle

Identifying the current phase of the family life cycle can readily be accomplished by ascertaining the ages and relationships of the family members living together under one roof. Knowing the stage the family has reached in its developmental cycle is an important anchoring point for a basic understanding of its structure and functioning, actual and optimal. This has been discussed at greater length in Chapters 2 and 3. Each stage of the family life cycle has unique stresses, challenges, opportunities, and pitfalls. By being alert to these, the therapist is in a position to observe and explore those particular tasks, roles, and relationships that are phase-specific for the family. The therapist can ascertain, too, to what extent the family members clearly recognize and are attempting to cope with actual issues relevant to the family's current stage of development. For many marriages and families, the basic difficulty underlying the need for professional help can be related to the family's inability to cope satisfactorily with its current developmental phase.

The J. family, mentioned in Chapter 3, was a good example of problems in a later stage of marriage—the "empty nest" syndrome—in

Table 2
Outline for Family Evaluation*

  I. Current Phase of Family Life Cycle

 II. Explicit Interview Data
    A. What is the current family problem?
    B. Why does the family come for treatment at this time?
    C. What is the background of the family problem?
      1. Composition and characteristics of nuclear and extended family, e.g., age, sex, occupation, financial status, medical problems, etc.
      2. Developmental background of husband and wife
      3. Courtship, marriage, and course of nuclear family
      4. Family relations (internal and external) prevailing at the time of first contact
    D. What is the history of past treatment attempts or other attempts at problem solving in the family?
    E. What are the family's goals and expectations of the treatment? What are their motivations and resistances?

III. Formulating the Family Problem Areas
    A. Family patterns of communicating thoughts and feelings
    B. Family roles and coalitions
    C. Operative family myths

IV. Planning the Therapeutic Approach and Establishing the Treatment Contract

---

*In developing this outline, we have adapted material from two major sources: (1) Gill M, Newman R, Redlich F: The Initial Interview in Psychiatric Practice. New York, International Universities Press, 1954; and (2) Group for the Advancement of Psychiatry. *The Case History Method in the Study of Family Process*, Report No. 76. New York, Group for the Advancement of Psychiatry, 1970.

which the family could not master the separation of the children because of the fear of the husband and wife of being alone together.

Explicit Interview Data

What is the current family problem? The interviewer asks this of each family member, in turn, with all family members present. The interviewer attempts to maintain the focus on the *current family problem,* rather than on one or another individual or on past difficulties. Each family member receives an equal opportunity to be heard, without interruption, and to feel that his opinions and views are worthwhile, important, and will be listened to. The interviewer will begin to note what frames of reference are delineated by the family members in discussing their difficulties, whether it is seen as a family or an individual problem, which individuals seem to be bearing the brunt of blaming, how the identified patient deals with his role, what the alliances in the family are, who seems to get interrupted by whom, who speaks for whom, who seems fearful or troubled about expressing an opinion, who sits next to whom, and so forth. (These issues and others are discussed more fully in Appendix A.)

Why does the family come for treatment at the present time? The answer to this question helps to move the focus of difficulty even more into the current situation and also provides an opportunity for making more specific the kinds of factors that lead to family distress. The kinds of "last straws" usually present the important patterns of family difficulty in microcosm.

In the L. family, a son, Tom, age 25, had symptoms of paranoid schizophrenia for many years. The parents "allowed" Tom to sleep in their bedroom at night. On the day after he moved out, Mr. and Mrs. L. began to feel that there was "real trouble" in the family, started to blame each other for the son's behavior, and sought attention because their son was "out on the streets and anything could happen." The son had maintained an uneasy balance between parents by staying in the parental bedroom at night, thus obviating intimacy or sex. It was only when he moved out that this came into sharp focus.

The answer to this question also helps alert the therapist to any acute crisis situation that may need his or the family's immediate intervention. It will be relevant, too, in assessing the goals the family has in mind for the therapy and the degree to which they are motivated for help.

What is the background of the family problem?
1. Composition and characteristics of nuclear and expanded family, including, age, sex, occupation, financial status, medical problems, and so on.
2. Developmental background of husband and wife.
3. Courtship, marriage, and course of nuclear family.
4. Family relations (internal and external) prevailing at the first contact.[1]

This part of the evaluation especially lends itself to being expanded or contracted depending upon the circumstances. For example, an intensive examination of a particular sector of the family's current functioning or past history might be thought relevant in a particular instance. In another situation, only a relatively brief amount of background data might be gathered intially, with the feeling that more would come out as the treatment sessions proceeded. At a minimum, one would want to ascertain the important participants in the family's current interactions, the quality of the relationships, and the developmental patterns of this family unit over time. For those interested in obtaining much more detailed family history and process data, a more extensive outline is provided in Appendix B.

What is the history of past treatment attempts or other attempts at problem solving in the family? It usually will be illuminating to understand the circumstances that led the marital couple or family to seek assistance in the past, from what sort of helpers this assistance was elicited, and what the expectations, experiences, and results turned out to be. Experience in previous help-seeking efforts serves to illuminate more clearly both the family processes and possible therapist-traps vs. useful strategies. Past help-seeking patterns are often useful predictors of what the present experience will be, in family therapy as in other therapies.

> The B. family came into treatment with the presenting complaint that they could not get along with each other and were contemplating divorce. They gave a history of being in family therapy several years before. They had had some 20 sessions, which "of course led to nothing." In discussion with the couple and with the former therapist, it was discovered that the couple had spent most of the sessions blaming each other and each attempting to change the other, rather than making any change in their relationship or in themselves. In addition, Mr. B., who was quite authoritarian, had gotten the therapist to line up on his side and say that his wife was "quite unreasonable." This treatment had been unsuccessful. The strategy in this case was to go over, in detail, the past problems in treatment, suggest that the therapist would not be a judge, and that the focus was their relationship. Each person would have to think what he or she could do to change the relationship rather than what "the other partner would *have* to do."

When one partner has been in individual psychotherapy or psychoanalysis, especially when the treatment is intensive (2, 3, 4, or even 5 times a week), and there has been no improvement in the relationship, a common outcome is for both therapist and patient to blame the failure in treatment on the spouse not in treatment. This usually exacerbates rather than alleviates the difficulty in the family and often will lead to separation or divorce. Mrs. P. was such a patient.

Mrs. P. came into treatment because she felt her husband was "inadequate." Her own life had been replete with difficulties, starting from the time she had lost both her parents in an automobile accident when she was 2. She lived in various orphanages, had two marriages by the time she was 22, and had periodic bouts of alcoholism and depression. She felt that her present marriage of 5 years was "OK" until she had children. She felt that although she had some difficulty in raising the children, the real problem was "in her husband." She went into individual psychotherapy 3 times a week, and in the course of this began to "see quite clearly what a loser he was." Although her therapist at first struggled valiantly to point out her own difficulties, he, too, began to see "the difficulties in the husband." The husband himself was never called into therapy and after some 2 years of treatment the couple was still experiencing the same problems and was referred by their minister for marital couple treatment.

What are the family's goals and expectations of the treatment? What are their motivations and resistances? Some families come to treatment for short-term goals, such as making final an already fairly well-decided separation between husband and wife. Others come for more long-term goals, such as making a basic change in how the family functions. Other families come because of "mother's depression" (an individual-oriented goal), while still others come because "the family isn't functioning right" (a family goal). In a case where the goals are individual-oriented, the therapist's task is to translate for the family the relationship between the symptoms and the family processes. At times, goals are unclear or unrealistic. In such instances, the therapist must work out with the family from the beginning an appropriate and clear set of goals (see Chapter 5).

The marital couple and family presumably will have certain types of positive hopes and motivations for seeking help, and at the same time will have some temptations, doubts, and fears about this very same help. One of the jobs of the therapist is to explore and reinforce the positive motivations, to clarify them, and keep them readily available throughtout the process of therapy, which at times may be temporarily stormy and stressful. Ideally, it would be desirable for each involved family member to know clearly what positive reasons there are for his own participation, as well as understanding what the more general family system goals may be. At the same time, the therapist must be aware of individual and family resistance to treatment, either in part or in whole, and where appropriate try to make explicit these obstacles and negative feelings before they undermine either the successful utilization of treatment or its actual continuance. Such resistances may be of various sorts. While some may be specific to particular families, many are very commonly seen. Among these are feelings that situations may be made worse by treatment, that someone will come to feel very guilty, depressed, angry, or fearful as a result of the treatment, that someone may go crazy, that the family may split up, that perhaps there is no hope for change and it is already too late for help, that someone may have to reveal shameful or damaging "family secrets," or that perhaps it would be better to stick to familiar patterns of family interaction, no matter how unsatisfying they may be, rather than attempt to change these, which leads in unknown and hence frightening directions. Chapter 9 is devoted to a more detailed review of resistance to treatment, including family secrets.

It is useful to try to give everyone in the family a chance to express what he or she would like to get out of the treatment experience in a positive sense. Equally important is for them to express what they may fear to be some negative results of seeking help. Obviously, the negatives must be kept in mind, as these may prevent the family's continuing in treatment or working very strongly at it. Clinical judgment will suggest when such fears and resistances need immediate attention and when they need only be kept in mind as potential major obstacles.

It is the positive expectations, goals, and motivations that keep the family members coming, and every effort should be made to insure that each family member will benefit from the family therapy sessions in some way individually, as well as in family-system terms. It has been found helpful to work out these expectations explicity, so that both the family members and the therapist understand them, in order to avoid a family member's having the feeling that he is attending the sessions not for himself, but only to help some other member of the family.

In the newlywed Q. family, the wife felt that to continue in marital treatment after her recovery from an acute psychotic episode might mean that she would go crazy again. She believed that she would have to explore with her husband their unsatisfactory marriage and that this might lead to separation or divorce. She also felt that she would have to be strong and powerful, to prevent her husband's committing suicide in the same way that his own father had committed suicide, presumably in relation to having had a weak, nonsupportive wife. The husband, for his part, was an advanced obsessional character with little interpersonal sensitivity or emotional awareness, who felt angry at psychiatrists and who felt insecure enough to be threatened by a therapist as a male role model.

Formulating the Family Problem Areas

When he is with the family, the therapist experiences their patterns of interaction and uses the data he obtains in order to begin formulating his concept of the family problem. Data for these hypotheses may come from historical material, but at least as important will be what the therapist himself has observed in his own contact with the family. This will help to form a basis for hypotheses and therapeutic strategies. (The four topics discussed below are discussed in greater detail in Chapter 7.)

The data gathered from the outline provided should permit the family therapist to pinpoint particular areas or aspects of the family that may require attention. In addition, they also lend themselves to being used to lay out a priority system, so that the therapist can begin to decide which areas of the family problem should be dealt with first, which later on. They also make possible greater clarity about therapeutic strategy and tactics indicated for the particular phases and goals of treatment.

Family patterns of communicating thoughts and feelings. Here will be noted such factors as general feeling tone of the family and of individual members, dyads, triads, and so forth, together with appropriateness, degree of variability, intensity, flexibility. To what extent does the family appear to be largely emotionally "dead," to what extent does there appear to be an emotional "divorce" between the marital partners? To what extent does the predominant family mood pattern seem to be one of anger, irritation, and frustration? To what extent is the family system "skewed" around the particular mood state or reaction pattern of one of its members? For example, in the X. family, whenever the son begins to hallucinate, the mother becomes angry and/or the father begins to withdraw. These and similar questions will be important in determining the extent of affective difficulty in the family system.

The variety of dysfunctional communication patterns and suggestions for dealing with them are presented in greater detail in Chapter 7.

Family roles and coalitions. To what extent does the family seem fragmented and disjointed, as though made up of isolated individuals? Or, does it rather appear to be one relatively undifferentiated "ego mass"? To what extent are there role differentiations within individuals, as well as between one individual and another? To what extent is the marital coalition the most functional and successful one in the family system? To what extent are there cross-generational dyadic coalitions that are stronger than the marital dyad? To what extent is this a "schismatic" family in which there are two or more alliances seemingly in continual conflict with one another? These and similar issues are discussed further in Chapter 7.

Operative family myths. Some individuals in families are elected to be "bad, sick, stupid, or crazy," and often these allocations constitute a kind of self-fulfilling prophecy. In addition, families as well as individuals function with a set of often largely unexamined philosophical attitudes that have been termed "myths." These markedly influence the family's coping ability and functional status. (These have been discussed in greater detail in Chapter 3.)

Planning the Therapeutic Approach and Establishing the Treatment Contract

After the evaluative data have been gathered and formulated into hypotheses and goals regarding important problem areas, the therapist is ready to consider what therapeutic strategies will be appropriate. (This subject is discussed in Chapters 5–12.)

At this point, a definite, clearly defined contract with regard to goals and treatment should be established. This should include: who is to be present; the location, time, estimated length, and frequency of meetings; the fee; and contingency planning with respect to absent members and missed appointments. Obviously, for some families treatment will be very brief and crisis oriented, lasting only one or two sessions, while for other families treatment may continue for years.

It may be helpful, at this point, for the therapist to make a concise, explicit statement of the family problem(s) couched in terms the family can understand. Such a statement can be used as a springboard for discussing the treatment plan. For example, the therapist might say, "I think that your drinking has to do with some of the feelings you and your wife have about each other. Perhaps it has to do with your feelings that she is trying to limit your 'fun.' She doesn't understand how hard you have to work. I think we should meet together to see how we can change things in the family and explore what happened."

The following case example will illustrate the use of the outline for family evaluation.

Case Study

I. **Current Phase of the Family Life Cycle**
The therapist notes: The patient is a 44-year-old white, female. Her husband is 55, and there are three children ranging in age from 17 to 22 years. This family is approaching the

empty nest phase, in which the parents will have to face the realization of being alone together. The therapist begins to ask himself to what extent the couple has put all of themselves in their children, rather than in the marital dyad, and to what extent this family has encouraged the development of the children's ability to move out of the house and complete their maturation and separation from the parents.

II. **Explicit Interview Data**
   A. *What is the current family problem?*
      The older son said that the family problem was his mother, since she had recently stopped using barbiturates on the advice of her doctor and subsequently began having ideas that people in the family were trying to harm her. The father added that his wife had always "been the problem." He was joined in these sentiments by his daughter, who is 17, and by the younger son, age 20. The mother, however, said that the problem was that nobody would help her or that she could not get any cooperation from the family members around the house.
      The therapist then asked the family to think in terms of what the current *family* (not individual) problem was. The younger son then said he thought that maybe the problem was not Mother, but the fact that nobody in the family was communicating, or even happy.
      The oldest son, who has been living in a room by himself in some other part of the house, is preparing to move out and to move in with his girlfriend. The arrangement had happened 7 days prior to the present admission.
   B. *Why does the family come for treatment at this time?*
      The family reported that about the time the older son announced that he was going to move out, the parents' quarreling intensified. The mother went to a family doctor for "a tranquilizer." He said that she appeared more confused, and suggested she stop taking the barbiturates she had been using. She then became even more suspicious and had a tremendous fight with her husband, including pot-throwing on both sides. At this point, everybody felt that they should see her family physician, who recommended an admission to an inpatient unit.
   C. *What is the background of the family problem?*
      1. Composition and characteristics of nuclear and extended family. The identified patient was a 44-year-old

white female housewife. Her husband was a 55-year-old white male who worked at manual labor in a shipyard. The older son was 22 and worked part time in a record store; the younger son was 20 and a student at college; there was a 17-year-old daughter.

2. Developmental background of husband and wife. Mrs. R.'s father was manager of a cemetery, and the patient describes her mother as being sick all the time. The parents' relationship revolved around the father's taking care of the mother through much of the marriage, because of her sickness. Mr. R's father was well liked but his "mother was an overprotective bitch," and the father essentially catered to his wife.

   Mrs. R. gave a history of being chronically sick. She had been born premature and developed sinusitis and asthma at an early age. She was the younger of two siblings, having an older brother.

   Mr. R. was the oldest of four sibs and took care of his two younger sibs who were always sick. He also had physical problems. He never quite lived up to his parents' expectations. He quit college, did not want to move out of the house, and dated very little.

3. Courtship, marriage, and course of nuclear family. The patient and her husband were introduced by relatives. Most of their courtship was involved with family-type social events, and there was very little intimacy or being alone during the courtship period. Mrs. R. described the marriage as somewhat disappointing. She indicated that she had married him for stability, while he had said that he thought "she would provide some of the spark" that he lacked. According to both parents, they had no knowledge of contraception or sex and a child was born early in the first year of the marriage. They had very little experience being alone together as husband and wife. After they had the other two children, the family pattern was that Mr. R. began spending more and more time at work. Mrs. R. found herself becoming "sicker and sicker with various respiratory as well as other ailments." They both had to turn to their own mothers, his for financial support, hers for support and help in raising the children and taking care of Mrs. R.

4. Family relations prevailing at the time of the first contact. At the time of the referral there had been progres-

sive worsening of the situation for the past 2 years. Husband and wife found themselves drifting further and further apart and spending less and less time together, barely talking. Mr. R. was working more and more and Mrs. R. was suspicious that he was "chasing around." Mrs. R. continued to have physical symptoms, took more and more medications, and became less and less able to do any child rearing or housekeeping. The older son began to experiment with the use of psychedelic drugs; the younger son had difficulty with his grades, and the daughter went to school less and less and did poorly. The two mothers-in-law fought over who was helping the family more, each placing the blame on the other's child.

D. *What is the history of past treatment attempts or other attempts at problem solving in the family?*

The mother had been seeing the same internist over the past 15 or 20 years. He had frequently suggested psychiatric treatment, but she had refused. She went for individual psychotherapy over a 3-month period but quit, saying, "It didn't make my husband better." They also consulted their local family clergyman on several occasions, and he "counseled tolerance and patience." Both Mrs. R. and the family did not find past treatment very helpful because it did not get to the "heart of the problems in the family" and because she seemed to be developing all kinds of "phony insights."

E. *What are the family's goals and expectations of the treatment? What are their resistances?*

The family's expectations at first were to help the mother so "she could get better." During this evaluation interview, as the therapist clarified and opened up some channels of communication that were not previously open, it became apparent that the father had abdicated his role as a parent and as a spouse. Secondly, the marital coalition was almost nonexistent; coalitions present were daughter and father on one side vs. younger son and mother. The older son had "in many ways withdrawn from the battle" by using "drugs to blot it all out of my mind."

The primary resistances that existed during this evaluation interview were the scapegoating of the mother, the resistance to changing themselves, resistances that were evident, for example, in the father's saying he could not get to treatment sessions because of his job, no matter what time was suggested for the meeting.

Although it was less apparent than the resistances, each person in the family did seem to recognize that there was something wrong with the overall functioning of the family and with individual members that could be worked on.

III. Formulating the Family Problem Areas

A. *Family patterns of communicating thoughts and feelings*

Once the therapist has obtained the basic data from the family, he formulates hypotheses as to how this family operates. The data for these hypotheses are derived both from historical material and from direct observation of the family.

The therapist here noted that the general emotional tone of the family was one of anger and frustration. The family had difficulty agreeing on anything, even a laundry list. That topic led to various arguments involving many members of the family. The main alignments and communication patterns seemed to focus around father and daughter vs. younger son and mother, with the older son being neutral mediator. There was little or no spontaneous interaction or communication between the husband and wife. Even when the therapist tried to get them to talk to each other, it was impossible, as the wife felt that the husband never listened to her and the husband felt his wife was always complaining and could not do anything. There was very little follow-up of communication from one person talking to another. The family seemed to be five people, each pulling in a different direction. There did not seem to be any continuity of communication or closure. It was noted that the main parental communication was non-verbal and consisted of the mother's clutching her stomach, grabbing her heart, rolling her head back as though she were about to have a stroke or a heart attack, at which point the father would move his chair back, further away from everyone in the family.

B. *Family roles and coalitions*

This family appeared to be a group of isolated individuals, each going in his own direction, with little or no functional interaction overall. The therapist noted Mrs. R., who is currently a daughter, wife, and mother, has been unable to move out of her family of origin to her present family. She seems almost childlike in her presentation and her functioning. She seems to be overly involved as a daughter and less involved as a wife and mother. At this point, there has been a reversal of generation roles, with the daughter running the household and doing the cleaning and cooking. The daughter is also fulfilling some sort of spouse role, in that father and daughter frequently "go to the movies," while the identified patient stays home with her "headaches." The husband is likewise very involved with his family of origin. He has essentially given up his role as husband and turned over the role as father to the older son, who has been managing the family finances, bringing in extra money, and making the kinds of family decisions that Mr. R. "used to make." This son seems to be the mediator, with all communication going through him. All fights seem to be resolved in "his court." However, at the same time, this seems to be taking a toll on him as he "has not found himself" and is having great difficulty in job decision or career choice. It becomes clear then, that this son's leaving home would be a grave crisis for the family. The strongest coalition in the family appeared to be father/daughter instead of the more usual husband/wife. All three children seemed somewhat at odds, but united in a struggle to prevent their parents from taking power.

C. *Operative family myths*

In this family, it appeared that the mother was the "sick one," the father was "helpless," the daughter was a "pest," the older son was the "mediator," and the younger son was the "noninvolved one."

The family operated under the family myth that a happy marriage is one in which there are no disagreements. Mrs. R. lived under the fantasy that everything 'should be rosy" and that any flaws or problems were to be avoided and not to be discussed. Secondly, Mrs. R. felt that both marital partners should be as unselfish as possible and felt that she had sacrificed her life for her children and husband. On the other hand, Mr. R. felt that he had "worked to the bone" to bring home the money to keep the family going, sacrificing everything for everyone else. Both were bitterly resentful of the nonresponse of the rest of the family to their sacrifices. Mrs. R. was the scapegoat in the family. Whenever anything went wrong everyone turned to her. If what she had done did not seem to be an adequate

explanation, an explantation was found taking into account
"past hurts." Positive feedback had been virtually abandoned in this family for years. Finally, and most importantly, Mrs. R. had felt all along that things would work if
she could just remake her husband to become a handsome
prince charming instead of the small, rotund, shy, withdrawn man that he was.

IV.   **Planning the Therapeutic Approach and Establishing the
Treatment Contract**

The first choice was a decision to approach this problem
from a family point of view rather than by treating Mrs. R., the
"identified patient," as an individual, isolated from her family.

The family seemed to be in a crisis, facing the threatened
imminent departure of the older son, who was the family
mediator. They seemed unable to resolve this separation, that
is, the empty nest phase. The father seemed to be chronically
weak and ineffective, and both the mother's and the father's
relationship with their own families of origin were still inappropriate. The basic strategy was to strengthen the marital coalition by increasing interaction between the marital dyad, by
attempting to decrease the inappropriate interaction between
these two people and their families of origin, and by attempting
to decrease the cross-generational ties between these two people and their children.

The family was seen together and the marital couple as a
dyad for many of the sessions, and for a time the children were
seen alone without the parents. The calculated decision was
made to exclude the in-laws from treatment and to encourage
the marital dyad to take over the parental role that they had
abrogated not only to the older son, but also to their own
parents. In the marital sessions, positive attention was given to
reinforcing communication patterns between husband and
wife, picking up emotional cues, responding to each other,
rather than the husband withdrawing or the wife somaticizing.

The mother was encouraged to take over the maternal
role, the father was encouraged to start making some decisions
and discussing them first with the mother. The older son was
steered toward his girlfriend and making a career choice, and
letting the father make the decisions he was not making. The
daughter was told to pick up on her failing school work and to
stop doing the housekeeping and the cooking.

SPECIFIC EVALUATION TECHNIQUES

Structured Interview[2]

This interesting evaluation technique is useful in both office and research situations. An extended discussion of the procedure will be found in Appendix A.

Psychological Testing

Psychological examinations of the family are of two types: those that are individual-oriented and those that are interpersonal-system–oriented. Those that are individual-oriented have the advantage of greater standardization and validity; however, they have the disadvantage of not measuring the crucial variables in family dynamics, that is, what the family system is like. Another problem with such testing is that there are no normative data now available on families so that they can be meaningfully compared.

A few investigators have adapted the TAT[3,4] and Rorschach[5] tests, originally designed for individual use, for family evaluation. The entire family, meeting together, is asked to look at the card, discuss their percepts with one another, and try to arrive at a common story or interpretation. As in individual testing, the *process* by which the family arrives at its interpretation is as carefully noted as the *content* of the interpretation itself. Others have reported notable success in being able to predict the nature of the identified patient's clinical psychiatric symptomatology from an examination of the psychological test protocols of the patient's parents, tested jointly, with the patient absent.[6]

A psychological test based on interpersonal dynamics that has been used in clinical practice for evaluative purposes is the Interpersonal Behavior Game-Test as devised by Ravich.[7] This test is set up with a model engine and one set of tracks on which to complete 20 "trips" for imaginary money. There are two players, usually marital partners. Neither can see the other's manipulation of his train but they can see each other and communicate if they wish. Score for the couple is based on what they decide to do and how they communicate. There can be a profit or loss for the couple, or a gain for one and a loss for the other. The situation is set up in such a way as to make it impossible for either side to win unless both parties communicate and cooperate. This is meant to simulate the reality of actual married life. The couple can be observed as to the nature of their interaction, particularly the degree of their competitiveness compared to their cooperativeness, and numerical scores can be assigned to these two items.

In the experience of most clinicians, routine psychological testing of the family has not been of major clinical usefulness in family therapy. This is because, at the present time, these procedures are too costly and time consuming and offer only a limited amount of additional information beyond that gained from a diagnostic interview. (Psychological tests are further discussed in Chapter 14.)

Home Visits[8,9,10]

Many family therapists find it useful to visit the family in its own home, with as many family members present as possible. Sometimes this is done only once, during the evaluation period. It may, however, be beneficial at any time, for example, when the therapist senses a gross discrepancy between the interactions he observes in the office sessions and the reports of what is taking place at home. The timing of the visit can vary depending on the purpose, that is, setting a base line or seeing changes. The main advantage is a better understanding of the interaction by seeing the family on "its own turf." A limitation is the time consumed in making the visit. Some family researchers have lived with a family for a period of several weeks, much as an anthropologist might do in an unfamiliar culture.

REFERENCES

1. Group for the Advancement of Psychiatry. The Case History Method in the Study of Family Process. Report No. 76. New York, Group for the Advancement of Psychiatry, 1970.
2. Watzlawick P: A structured family interview. Family Process 5:256–271, 1966.
3. Winter W D, Ferreira A J, Olson J L: Hostility themes in the family TAT. Journal of Projective Techniques and Personality Assessment 30:270–275, 1966.
4. Winter W D, Ferreira A J, Olson J L: Story sequence analysis of family TAT's. Journal of Projective Techniques and Personality Assessment 29:392–397, 1965.
5. Willi J: Joint Rorschach testing of partner relationships. Family Process 8:64–78, 1969.
6. Jackson D D, Riskin J, Satir V: A method of analysis of a family interview. Arch Gen Psychiatry 5: 321–339, 1961.
7. Ravich R: Game-testing in conjoint marital psychotherapy. Am J Psychotherapy 23:217–229, 1969.
8. Fisch R: Home visits in a private psychiatric practice. Family Process 3:114–126, 1964.

9. Friedman A S: Family therapy as conducted in the home. Family Process
     1:132–140, 1962.
10. Henry J: The study of families by naturalistic observation, in Cohen I M
     (ed): Family Structure, Dynamics and Therapy. Psychiatric Research
     Report No. 20. New York, American Psychiatric Association, 1966, pp
     95–104.

5

Goals of Family Treatment

OBJECTIVES

- To conceptualize the different types of general goals of family therapy
- To apply these general goals of family treatment to specific families

The therapist, from his evaluation of what he hears and sees of the family's history and interactions, forms a concept of the family's difficulties (see Chapter 4). He often begins the treatment with what seems at the outset to be most crucial to the family and helps them to deal with whatever may appear to them to be an immediate crisis situation. Only after some stability and rapport have been achieved is it usually possible for the therapist to begin to help move the family into areas that he feels will be most beneficial. The work is often slow and gradual; sudden "miraculous" major shifts in longstanding family patterns are not likely to occur. When such rapid changes do occur, they often prove to be mirages and harbingers of later difficulty.

It will be helpful to think not only of the family as a whole and of the various interpersonal components (dyads, triads, and so forth), but also of the individuals who make up the system. Each will have his or her own history, personality, coping mechanisms. A thorough knowledge of individual personality theory and psychopathology is essential for knowing what to expect from the separate "atoms" as well as from the family "molecule."

At times it will be necessary to provide specific treatment for, or to direct specific attention to, the needs of an individual family member (for example, when one family member is floridly psychotic) with individual sessions, somatic treatment, and sometimes hospitalization (see Chapter 10).

But even under more usual circumstances, a thorough understanding of the strengths and weaknesses of each family member (basic personality patterns, reactions to stress, and so on) will help to determine the goals and techniques of the family therapy.

The goals of family treatment must be in some way congruent with what the family members seem to desire and what they are realistically capable of achieving at any particular point. However, the therapist's views of the appropriate therapeutic possibilities may differ from those the family members initially envisage. Overall goals often encompass the entire family system as well as the individual members thereof. Ideally, as a result of family therapy the entire family should function more satisfactorily, and each family member should derive personal benefit from the experience and results of the therapy. The family therapist, for example, should not be in the position of taking the focus off the scapegoated member (saying, "It's not Dad's drinking that is the problem") only to consistently seem to put the burden on one or another family member ("It's Mom's yelling") as the cause of the family's difficulties.

Traditionally, families enter therapy because of gross symptomatic difficulty. Often this is related to one family member. A marital partner may blame the spouse for causing his distress, or the wife may feel guilty because the children are not behaving properly. A child may be singled out as the "only problem" in the family. One member already may have been labelled, either inside the family or by some social agency, as being bad, sick, stupid, or crazy, and may enter the family treatment sessions as "the identified patient."

Less commonly, family members talk about system difficulties as such, "marital troubles," "family unhappiness." One family member may have instigated the seeking of help or, less frequently, the family as a whole has discussed the difficulties and has agreed to seek professional assistance. Families may come more or less on their own with varying degrees of motivation and expectations, or may be referred *in toto* by other agencies or individuals.

However, some families today are seeking professional help not for these more traditional reasons, but rather for clarification of family goals and an enhancing "growth experience." In such cases, a problem solving model seem less appropriate than a growth development model.

The goals of treatment will be related to what has been established during the initial evaluation period, as well as whatever develops as therapy progresses. All specific goals need not be explicitly spelled out at the onset of treatment; sometimes goals are left somewhat general, with specifics being clarified only later on or perhaps never being discussed explicitly. The particular areas to be dealt with, as well as a determination of the priority of dealing with them, must be carerfully considered. Some family therapists are relatively comfortable allowing goals to develop as therapy proceeds. Such treatment sometimes appears as a sequence of short-term problem resolutions. Other therapists attempt to delineate major goals early in the course of treatment or to get the family to cope better with problems that cannot be reversed, such as death of a family member.

One convenient way to conceptualize the categories of marital and family therapy goals is indicated below. It is based essentially on the categories presented in the preceding three chapters. These are relatively broad areas that allow for considerable flexibility according to the specifics of each particular marital or family unit. They are not mutually exclusive but are often intermixed. They (or other types of conceptualizations) are of use because they help clarify the therapist's idea of what he is trying to do, and they suggest potential treatment techniques and end results for evaluation. These general goals are

1. *To facilitate communication of thoughts and feelings.* The therapist utilizes his skills to aid the family members in the process of open, direct, gratifying, and meaningful communication. He clarifies blurred or ambiguous thoughts. He is also involved in fostering improved empathy between family members, diminishing the atmosphere of "emotional divorce" and bringing to the surface those buried feelings that are obstructing a more functional family interaction.

2. *To shift disturbed, inflexible roles and coalitions.* This may include helping to improve the autonomy and individualization of family members, to facilitate the more flexible assumption of leadership by any particular family member as circumstances require, and to facilitate the general task performance by one or more members.

3. *To serve as role model, educator, and demythologizer.* By his own example and by what he says, the therapist helps to change family patterns. When successful, these strategies will have the general effects of reducing the quarreling and conflict within the family, symptomatically improving one or more family members, increasing agreement about roles taken by family members, and enabling the family unit to continue to develop and grow.[1]

In family therapy, as in individual psychotherapy, questions are raised as to the relative importance of the *process* of therapy and the *content* of the therapy. The more traditional view tends to deal with substantive content issues, whereas the newer holistic systems-view looks more closely at the characteristic patterning in this interpersonal network, with less emphasis on the subject matter being dealt with. In some ways this may be an artificial dichotomy. For example, the communicational processes may become the most important "subject matter" of the therapy. Any attempt at dealing with a specific content issue inevitably brings to the surface "process issues."

Sometimes major emphasis is placed on a particular process technique and goal, such as straightening out a family's communicational patterns,[2] or helping family members deal with their feelings.[3] Family therapists, either on ideological grounds or because of the appropriateness to a particular family, may see such process goals as being primary, with the family then being left to deal with any and all content issues as it will, once having learned the general process paradigm. Other family therapists, perhaps because of differing conceptual bases applicable to different types of family goals, will tend to work in the other direction, that is, from the more specific content issues toward the more general process issues.

Many family therapists have adapted some of the techniques of individual and group psychotherapy, social case work, and individual counseling to their work with families. Although the family therapy field represents a different way of looking at and conceptualizing what transpires between people, in many ways some of the specific therapeutic practices of more traditional interpersonal helping procedures are useful in treating families. For example, the three general strategies enumerated above would not be altogether unfamiliar to the person engaged in treating individuals. However, the family therapist utilizes them in particular ways and in a particular setting.

Each of these strategies entails the use of a repertory of intervention tactics designed to produce the desired goal. These strategies are not based on any generally agreed upon theory of family structure, function, and therapy, but represent ad hoc attempts by clinicians to deal with the kinds of problems with which they are presented. Some family therapists believe strongly in one or another of these strategies and the concepts underlying them, and utilize the same basic strategy with every family. Others feel that one strategy may be particularly well suited to one type of family, while a different strategy is more appropriate for another sort of family. Still other therapists move flexibly from one to another of these strategies as the situation in any one family at any one time seems to require.[4]

These differences in outlook and practice can be bewildering to the inexperienced therapist who is not aware of the underlying rationale and indications. Given the current state of the field, with no unifying theory of family pathology, nomenclature, or theory of treatment, each new situation represents, in one sense, an "experiment" and requires checking the therapist's hypotheses.

REFERENCES

1. Sluzki C: A strategy for research in family therapy. Paper presented at the Langley Porter Neuropsychiatric Institute Noon Conference, December 13, 1972.
2. Satir V: Conjoint Family Therapy: A Guide to Theory and Technique. Palo Alto, Ca, Science and Behavior Books, 1964, pp 162–167, 175–176.
3. Paul N L: The role of mourning and empathy in conjoint marital therapy, in Zuk G H, Boszormenyi-Nagy I (eds): Family Therapy and Disturbed Families. Palo Alto, Ca, Science and Behavior Books, 1967, pp 186–205.
4. Group for the Advancement of Psychiatry. The Field of Family Therapy. Report No. 78. New York, Group for the Advancement of Psychiatry, 1970, pp 581–593.

6

Family Treatment: General Considerations

OBJECTIVES

- To be aware of, in general, which family participants to include in treatment and, specifically, indications and contraindications for including children, adolescents, grandparents, and significant others
- To know the advantages and disadvantages of various therapist combinations
- To be aware of the variety of settings in which family therapy has been used
- To be aware of types of scheduling of sessions in family therapy
- To consider the indications and contraindications of family therapy in combination with other treatments
- To know and be able to manage the pitfalls of family treatment in combination with other helping people and agencies

By this time, the reader will have some understanding of how families function and how their difficulties may be conceptualized. In addition, material has been presented relating to evaluating troubled famili~ setting appropriate goals. The following discussion con eral features of marital and family treatment, namely, the setting, the scheduling of treatment, and the use of fa combination with other treatment methods and helping a

FAMILY PARTICIPANTS

In practice it is often preferable to begin by seeing the entire family together. The family can be defined as broadly as one likes, to include, for example, all persons living under the same roof, all those persons closely related to one another, even though they do not necessarily live under the same roof (this might include, for example, in-laws) or, even more broadly, all persons significant to the family, even though not related to them (friends, "caretakers" or "social network").[1,2]

Sometimes family therapy is carried out with the same therapist meeting both with the whole family and with each family member individually (*concurrent family therapy*). At other times, two therapists who maintain some contact with one another, but who do not work jointly, may each see one or more members of a family (*collaborative family therapy*). *Conjoint family therapy* has been defined as family therapy in which the participants include at least two generations in a family, such as parents and children, plus the therapist, all meeting together. *Conjoint marital therapy* is similar but is limited to the two spouses plus the therapist.[3]

The question is often raised whether sessions should be conducted *only* when all family members are present. While from a certain absolutist point of view this may seem desirable, in actual practice this may be impossible or, at times, actively contraindicated. For example, it would seem more appropriate when investigating the sexual adjustment of the parents that the children usually not be present, unless there is some particular reason for them to participate. Often, too, the therapist will be involved with incomplete families, either because the family itself has experienced divorce or death, or because one or more family member temporarily or permanently refuses to participate. In the latter case, a decision will have to be made either at the outset or following the evaluation as to whether it is worthwhile and possible to continue working with the incomplete family.

At times individuals in the family will, for one reason or another, feel unused to or uncomfortable with talking about certain topics in front of the other family members. In such instances the family therapist will have to use his judgment as to when individual interviewing might be indicated. This might be done, for example, with the goal in mind of eventually bringing the material from the individual session, if possible and appropriate, to the entire family group. But it must be recognized that there may be family secrets that cannot be profitably shared with other family members and that must be kept private between an individual family member and the therapist. On these topics no rigid guidelines can be established, and it is here that there is no substitute for clinical judgment d experience.

Rather than specifying who should be included, one might say that the family concept can be extended to cover, when appropriate, other groups having an impact on the individuals concerned. These might be friends, relatives, people in professional helping or custodial roles, and so forth. These other relationship groups often do not have the same kind of impact and emotional hold, either in the past, present, or future, as do the individual's natural family. But at any particular time these groups of "significant others" may be quite important.

Extended Family and Significant Others

Family therapists include grandparents (or in-laws) as participants when they seem significant in the family difficulties. The question of whether or not to include a friend, fiancée, boyfriend, or girlfriend occasionally is raised. Such individuals should be included if their interaction seems important to the progress of the therapy. It should be pointed out that the techniques of family therapy seem *not* to have the same effect on such individuals as on family members. For example, pointing out a piece of disruptive behavior to a fiance of a family member ("You seem to encourage Carol to quit all her jobs.") may lead him to sever the relationship with the family member. They are also less motivated to change than are family members and are more likely to drop out of family therapy.

Young Children

With respect to the possible inclusion of infants and children, the decision would depend on the therapist's evaluation of the goals to be achieved. Many therapists prefer to include everyone in the household, including infants (and perhaps even pets!) during the evaluation period in order to observe how family members relate to one another. After the initial evaluation is completed, the therapist must decide whether the continued inclusion of an infant or nonverbal child tends more to aid or to disrupt the work of therapy.

Most family therapists probably would agree that infants and children should be included at least once for diagnostic purposes, and also that there are some issues between husband and wife that should be discussed with the children absent. Certainly much can be gained from having children present for most of the sessions, if for no other reason than that often they tend to be more open and direct than adults and will say what they think.

When young children are present, the parents are expected to exert control over them. If not, the therapist must take over and set a model. The therapist explains "special rules of the house." There is no destroying equipment, and everyone has a chance to be heard. The therapist must decide on how to handle requests to go to the toilet and for drinks of water. Another helpful idea is to keep the sessions short and provide material for play, such as toys, paper, and crayons.

Bell,[4] talking about the general process of therapy, has made some pertinent comments about children. He first meets with parents, alone, in order to explain the basis of family therapy. Then he meets with children and parents together and orients them. He explains that the children have a voice in what is said, and that the parents are expected to listen and not to talk while the children are talking. He calls this the "parent-child phase." He then moves into the parent phase, during which problems of the parents are explored. During this time, the children, as they gain trust in the therapist, are usually more active. In the terminal phase, the identified patient is more active in the family, in a more constructive way. Bell's experience concurs with ours that most "forbidden" topics usually have been heard already by the children.

Adolescents

Another interesting question concerns the inclusion of adolescents. On the one hand, they will often be crucially involved in the family unit's concerns and interactions. From this aspect, they should be included so that intergenerational conflicts and inadequate communication can be dealt with. On the other hand, one of the primary tasks of the adolescent, especially of the late adolescent, is to achieve increasing psychosocial autonomy from his family of origin. If adolescents are consistently included in all family sessions, there is a structural reinforcement of their solid entrenchment (or enmeshment) in all of the family's difficulties, and little recognition of the concerns that the marital pair, as a unit, needs to deal with, separate from their children. Thus, it may be indicated to have some sessions or a series of sessions in which only husband and wife are seen, with children absent. Sessions or parts of sessions may be devoted to seeing an adolescent alone, for the special purpose of reinforcing recognition of increasing autonomy. Of course, conjoint sessions also can be successfully used to explore issues of differentness and separation.

Obviously, careful recognition must be given to the readiness and ability of both the adolescent and his or her family to separate. Although individual autonomous functioning is seen in general as a desirable goal, there will be situations in which the therapist must be realistic with respect to the autonomous potential of adolescents suffering from brain damage, chronic schizophrenia, and so forth.

THERAPIST COMBINATIONS

Most family therapists operate as one therapist seeing one family. However, a number of therapists prefer to work with a *cotherapist*. The rationale has been that there is so much going on that two heads operate better than one and that one operates as a check on the other. For training purposes, it may be helpful to have a student therapist work with a more seasoned veteran.

On the other hand, some authors have found that cotherapists cause additional problems that can impede progress. For example, if the male therapist has had significant problems with his mother and treats a family that has a "difficult" mother, a female therapist might be difficult for him to work with effectively.

Cotherapists are usually of opposite sexes. The advantage of this is to give each family member someone of the same sex to identify with and to use as a model.

Another technique is to use different therapists not only for each individual family member, but also for the whole family together. This method has been used as part of Multiple Impact Therapy.[5]

One report has suggested the use of the *therapist and his family* to treat the identified patient and his family.[6] This must be considered experimental at this time.

The significant issues seem to be the use of the therapist's time and whether or not the therapist can work effectively with a cotherapist. A recent study[7] suggested that therapist satisfaction with a cotherapist decreases as experience in family therapy increases. Another obvious reason for the more common use of a single therapist is that it costs less.

SETTING

Family therapy has been done in settings such as child guidance clinics, psychiatric emergency rooms (walk-in or crisis clinics), psychiatric outpatient clinics, juvenile probation offices, domestic relations courts, psychiatric hospitals, medical offices, schools,[8] social welfare services,[9] and many other places. Entire families have been hospitalized for treatment purposes[10] and for research purposes.[11] Other family therapists have done family therapy in the home.[12-15] Advantages and disadvantages of home visits have been discussed in Chapter 4.

SCHEDULING

Most family therapists will see a family once a week, for an average of 50 to 90 minutes. Ninety minutes gives a chance for more things to happen and develop. A minority of therapists sees a family more than once a week. In inpatient settings, in general, family sessions may run longer. In times of crisis, the therapist should not hesitate to see the family more frequently. There is nothing sacred about once a week scheduling.

In "Multiple Impact Therapy" (MIT),[5] families are seen on an intensive basis in different combinations—mother-son, whole family, and so on—over a 2- or 3-day period by various members of a therapy team, consisting of psychiatrist, psychologist, social worker, and vocational counselor. Techniques focus on bringing about change in the family during this time period, since they have come for therapy from distant locations. A variant of this technique is that employed by Masters and Johnson[16] in their sex counseling, which consists of a 2-week course of treatment with multiple daily sessions with one male and one female cotherapist.

The decision as to the overall duration of treatment would depend, among other factors, on the goals of treatment (see Chapter 5).

RELATIONSHIP OF FAMILY THERAPY
TO OTHER THERAPIES

At present, the differential effectiveness of family therapy alone or in combination with other therapies is not known. Therefore, each therapist must "play it by ear." Most therapists use family therapy in combination with other therapies (somatic, individual, group, and so forth).

A minority of family therapists uses conjoint family therapy alone. By this is meant that there is no other treatment used, including individual therapy. All contacts are kept strictly within the joint family setting, and the therapist will not communicate even by telephone with individual family members. The rationale is to avoid any type of coalition derived from material shared by the therapist and only part of the family system.

There have been a number of different combinations of family therapy in conjunction with other treatment methods. First, there is individual psychotherapy plus family therapy.[17] The two types of therapy can be carried out by the same therapist or by different therapists. If the therapist is the same for both the individual and the family psychotherapy, the therapist has the advantage of knowing both the individual and the family. On the other hand, this combination changes the nature of the therapy as follows: (1) the patient in individual therapy feels that what he reveals in the one-to-one situation may in some way (either overtly or covertly) be communicated to the family by the therapist; (2) family members may be reluctant to deal with sensitive issues in the conjoint sessions, preferring to reveal them in individual sessions; and (3) transference in individual therapy does not develop as fully, since the patient can express directly his feelings about his family in the family therapy. This may present an unsurmountable obstacle to the individual therapy. Another disadvantage is that inexperienced therapists tend to identify with the individual patient, seeing the family from the "patient's" point of view. That is, the therapist, to use an extreme example, may see all problems as resulting from "this cold, passive, authoritarian father and smothering, double-binding, rejecting mother" and what they have done to the "poor patient." This makes it extremely difficult to work with the whole family in conjoint therapy.

Individual therapy has been done with mother and/or father individually, plus the family. It has also been done with mother and/or child individually, and it has been done for all family members individually (an approach employed commonly in child psychiatric practice).

Family therapy has been prescribed in combination with group therapy[18,19] and with behavioral therapy.[20,21] It has also been used in conjunction with hospitalization for one member (usually the identified patient) or for all members of the family in both inpatient[11,22] and day hospital[23] settings. It also has been prescribed in conjunction with psychopharmacological medications[24] and with electric shock therapy, the rationale being that in order for family therapy to be done, the identified patient's acute symptoms must be controlled.

Family therapy has also been prescribed as an adjunct to other therapies: for example, when individual therapy[25] or psychoanalysis[26] is the primary therapy. The rationale is that it is useful for diagnostic purposes to correct "distorted" impressions, and to shorten treatment.[26] See Chapter 1 for indications and comparisons of several types of psychosocial treatments.

FAMILY THERAPY IN COMBINATION WITH OTHER HELPING AGENCIES AND THERAPIES

The family therapist often finds himself in the situation of using family therapy at the same time that other helping agencies are also exerting influences on the family. This gives added help, but also creates multiple problems and pitfalls.

In some families there is simultaneous medical treatment for one or more members of the family. Such medical treatment may exert a significant influence on the family[27] which, in some cases, in the judgment of the family therapist, may make things worse. For example, one family member may be receiving cortisone for rheumatoid arthritis, which may make that member euphoric. He may be difficult for the family to live with. The family therapist will have to be in continuing contact with the family physician to coordinate treatment in such cases.

More commonly, families have multiple problems that involve a wide variety of agencies: welfare, probation, school, housing, and so on. These agencies may be pulling in different directions. The first task is to decide "who's in charge." If the family therapist is in charge, it will be his job to coordinate the various agencies in the service of the family's goals. Much duplication, wasteful effort, inefficiency, and impediments to the progress of the family can be so avoided.

Finally, the family therapist should be alert to the possibility that family members may play off one agency against the other in the service of their needs. For example, the family may want the identified patient (son) not to function so he can get welfare or disability payments, whereas the therapist's goal is for the son to function at a job. Another example is when a family insists that the identified patient be in good enough shape so that he can get his disability certification renewed, but not in such good shape that it would be taken away. In another case, a spouse who is not getting along with her husband may suggest to the probation worker that the husband has been violating his parole and should go back to jail, whereas she tells the family therapist that she is trying to work out their problems to stay together.

REFERENCES

1. Speck R V, Rueveni U: Network therapy: A developing concept. Family Process 8:182–191, 1969
2. Speck R V, Attneave C: Network therapy, in Haley J (ed): Changing Families. New York, Grune & Stratton, 1971, pp 312–332.
3. Cutter A V, Hallowitz D: Diagnosis and treatment of the family unit with respect to the character-disordered youngster. Journal of the American Academy of Child Psychiatry 1:605–618, 1962.
4. Bell J E: Family Group Therapy. Public Health Monograph No. 64. Washington, D. C.: Department of Health, Education and Welfare, Public Health Service, 1961.
5. MacGregor R, Ritchie A M, Serrano A C, Schuster F P, McDanald E C,

Goolishian H A: Multiple Impact Therapy With Families. New York, McGraw-Hill, 1964.

6. Landes J, Winter W: A new strategy for treating disintegrating families. Family Process 5:1–20, 1966.
7. Rice D, Fey W, Kepecs J: Therapist experience and "style" as factors in co-therapy. Family Process 11:227–238, 1972.
8. Moss S: School experiences as family crisis. Journal of the International Association of Pupil Personnel Workers 15:115–121, 1970.
9. Morris R: Welfare reform 1973: The social services dimension. Science 181:515–522, 1973.
10. Abrams G, Fellner C, Whitaker C: The family enters the hospital. Am J Psychiatry 127:1363–1370, 1971.
11. Bowen M: Family psychotherapy. Am J Orthopsychiatry 31:40–60, 1961.
12. Friedman A S: Family therapy as conducted in the home. Family Process 1:132–140, 1962.
13. Speck R V: Family therapy in the home. Journal of Marriage and the Family 26:72–76, 1964.
14. Speck R V: Family therapy in the home, in Ackerman N (ed): Expanding Theory and Practice in Family Therapy. New York, Family Service Association of America, 1967, pp 39–46.
15. Fisch R: Home visits in a private psychiatric practice. Family Process 3:114–126, 1964.
16. Masters W, Johnson V: Human Sexual Response. Boston, Little, Brown, 1966.
17. Greene B L (ed): The Psychotherapies of Marital Disharmony. New York, Free Press, 1965.
18. Leichter E, Shulman G: The family interview as an integrative device in group therapy with families. International Journal of Group Psychotherapy 13:335–345, 1963.
19. MacGregor R: Group and family therapy: Moving into the present and letting go of the past. International Journal of Group Psychotherapy, 20: 495–515, 1970.
20. Fine S: Family therapy and behavioral approach to childhood obsessive-compulsive neurosis. Arch Gen Psychiatry 28:695–697, 1973.
21. Coe W: Behavioral approach to disrupted family interactions. Psychotherapy: Theory, Research and Practice 9:80–85, 1972.
22. Fleck S: Some general and specific indications for family therapy. Confin Psychiatr 8:27–36, 1965.
23. Zwerling I, Mendelsohn M: Initial family reactions to day hospitalization. Family Process 4:50–63, 1965.
24. Cohen M, Freedman N, Engelhardt D, Margolis R A: Family interaction patterns, drug treatment, and change in social aggression. Arch Gen Psychiatry 19:1950–1956, 1968.
25. Szalita A: The combined use of family interviews and individual therapy in schizophrenia. Am J Psychotherapy 22:419–430, 1968.
26. Szalita A: The relevance of the family interview for psychoanalysis. Contemporary Psychoanalysis 8:31–44, 1971.
27. Anthony E: The impact of mental and physical illness on family life. Am J Psychiatry 127:138–146, 1970.

7

Family Treatment:
Specific Strategies

OBJECTIVES

- To become familiar with three broad family treatment strategies and their application in various specific situations

The specific treatment strategies to be discussed here follow from the material presented in the chapters on evaluation and goals (Chapters 4 and 5). Family therapists ultilize one or another of these strategies in their treatment plans. Some therapists prefer to operate with one strategy in most cases (for example, the "communication theory" therapists), whereas others intermix these strategies depending on the type of case and the phase of treatment. At times the type of strategy used is made explicit by the therapist, while in other instances it remains implicit or covert. But irrespective of whether a therapist "specializes" in one or another approach, or whether he is "eclectic," he *must* form some hypotheses about the nature of the family's difficulty and the approach he will adopt.

Family therapy is an active process. The therapist is in charge. However, it must be pointed out that the family sets the pace as to how fast the therapy progresses.

The therapist is a participant-observer. He characteristically moves in and out of the therapeutic process. He is active, open, sometimes blunt, and confident. He is optimistic (in contrast to the pessimism of the family usually encountered). He is fluid and flexible.

The therapist makes use of the family's positive feelings toward him to further the work of treatment, and will take up only those personal attitudes toward him that seem to be obstructing progress. For example, the mother may relate negatively to the therapist and to her husband in a way similar to her relationship with her father.

Three major therapeutic strategies have been signled out for detailed discussion:

- The therapist facilitates communication of thoughts and feelings.
- The therapist attempts to shift disturbed, inflexible roles and coalitions.
- The therapist functions as a family role model, educator and demythologizer.

THE THERAPIST FACILITATES COMMUNICATION
OF THOUGHTS AND FEELINGS

The therapist is an expert in communication and helps the family members express their thoughts and feelings more clearly to one another. He tries to promote open and clear communication, emotional empathy, and positive rapport between family members. He knows that disturbed families often have major problems in this regard.[1,2] For example, while it is impossible *not* to communicate in a family, nevertheless in many troubled families, members spend very little time talking meaningfully with one another. Not only thoughts, but feelings, too, are distorted, "hidden," negative or blurred. The therapist supplies an arena for family discussion. He is aware of the different levels of meaning in messages and how these influence and sometimes contradict each other. He is sensitive to "doublebinds"[3,4] and discourages one family member's "reading" another's mind or acting as "spokesman" for someone else. He does not allow anyone to monopolize the session, nor does he allow anyone to speak for someone else. At the same time, he attempts to encourage interpersonal sensitivity and empathy, and tries to help each person become more aware of his own thoughts and feelings.

The therapist encourages family members to speak using nouns —who did what to whom, for example, "Dad took my book from Aunt," rather than "He took it." Individuals are held accountable for their actions. The therapist fills in gaps in communication. He points out discrepancies. He deals with nonverbal communication.[5] The therapist points out nonproductive verbal and nonverbal family communication patterns. He tries to identify the implicit, unstated patterns or attitudes that may be causing trouble. He makes overt what is covert. He makes explicit what is implicit. He opens up blocked channels of communication and feeling.[6] Good communication includes listening. Often three or four family members are heard talking at exactly the same time, presumably so as to avoid hearing thoughts and feelings other than their own. The therapist, in such a situation, may function as a communications traffic cop or referee.

The therapist may use a number of techniques common to all forms of psychotherapy, such as confrontation (that is, pointing out patterns to the family, for example, "I notice that whenever your son steals a car, you beat up your wife"); support ("I can understand how hard you have tried to be good parents."), interpretation (that is, pointing out the why's of behavior, for example, to a father, "I notice that whenever you beat up your wife, it is as if you are beating up your mother"), and other techniques. A unique advantage of family therapy is that when an interpretation does not work because of one or more family members' resistance to the *therapist*, the therapist can allow or even encourage another family member to make the interpretation. A family member (for example, a child) may "hear" an interpretation from another member (a sibling) that he will not accept from the therapist.

The therapist decreases threat by reducing the need for defensiveness. He helps bring both positive and negative feelings into the open. He will try to decrease the atmosphere of "emotional divorce," meaninglessness, nonproductive conflict and arguing, endless recriminations and blaming, and pseudoagreement. He may need to bring to the surface long-buried feelings that are obstructing the family's current functioning.[7]

On the other hand, he may need to handle emotionally charged material carefully. This can be done by support, switching subjects, generalizing, changing the temporal focus, and so forth, until the family is ready to deal with a particular issue. He can use a variety of techniques to help the family to take distance from emotionally charged material—for example, helping the family members to laugh at themselves.

He may try to bring out in the open both the interpersonal and individual conflicts that are causing family problems. For example, a father who hates his own mother may set up situations where he is in continuous conflict with his own wife, not only because of his previous conflicts with his mother, but also because of some of his wife's problems, and these may be displaced onto other female members of the family. Usually, there is more emphasis on interpersonal relationships than on individual processes.

The N. family consisted of father, mother, two adolescent boys, and a 7-year-old girl. In this family, the father spoke to his wife as though he were running his plant. He expected her to listen because he was "the boss." He would say to her, "you take out the garbage, prepare the supper, and get things ready for the weekend." She would sit looking out the window, and when he would really yell at her she would begin to cry. The therapist questioned whether either of them was aware of what the other was feeling or thinking. Neither of them was able to state with any assurance that he or she knew what was happening with the other. The children meanwhile would laugh while this was going on. The therapist's intervention was to have each parent say what he or she expected or wanted to do, and how he or she would do it. The attempt was to get both partners to work out a *modus operandi*. Several times the therapist commented that the father seemed to be reacting to the mother as though she were an employee at his plant. He seemed totally unable to hear this until the 7-year-old said to him, "Daddy, Mommy doesn't work for you." He then appeared surprised. Subsequently he began to be able to increase his awareness of the effect on his wife of this authoritarian manner.

THE THERAPIST ATTEMPTS TO SHIFT DISTURBED, INFLEXIBLE ROLES AND COALITIONS

A graphic representation of some family coalitions is provided in Figure 2. A "typical" four-member family is taken as the unit, with the squares representing the males and the circles, females. The larger symbols stand for spouse/parent, and the smaller symbols represent the offspring/siblings, respectively. The solid straight lines joining these symbols are intended to represent positive communicational, emotional, and activity bonds between the individuals involved, with a semi-quantitative indication according to the number of straight lines utilized. Dotted lines, on the other hand, are meant to represent the relative absence of or relatively negatively tinged tone to the interactions.

Turning first to Example A, the Functional Family, we see the marital coalition as the strongest pathway in the family, with all other channels open and about equal to each other in importance.

In contrast are the various types of dysfunctional families. In Example B, the marital coalition is relatively weak or absent, and instead there are strong alliances across the generations and sexes, between father and daughter, and between mother and son. Other channels are relatively unavailable. In Example C, we have a somewhat similar type, except that the cross-generational ties are between father and son and mother and daughter, with relative absence of other effective channels. Examples B

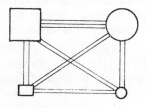

A. Functional

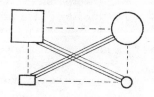

B. Schismatic

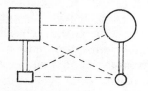

C. Schismatic

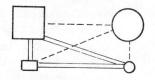

D. Skewed

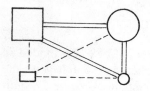

E. Skewed

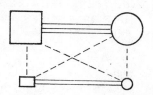

F. Generation gap

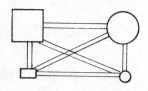

G. Pseudodemocratic

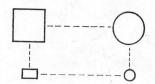

H. Disengaged

Fig. 2. Types of Family Coalitions

and C can be thought of as representations of simple forms of the Schismatic Family.

In Examples D and E we have one family member relatively isolated from the other three, who form a fairly cohesive unit. One might think of such units as Skewed Families. Example F represents the family suffering from excessive Generation Gap, in which the marital unit and the offspring each form a fairly cohesive duo, with little or no interaction across the generational lines. Example G represents the Pseudodemocratic Family, in which all channels seem to be of about equal importance, with the marital coalition and the parental role not being particularly well differentiated. Example H, the Disengaged Family, offers the representation of an extreme case in which each family member is pretty much cut off from every other member, and in which one would expect very little sense of positive interaction or feeling of belonging to a family unit.

Clearly, these representations are highly oversimplified, and are pictured only for a two-generation, four-member family. Infinite variety could be added to the list. The major point, however, would be that such representation enables the therapist to conceptualize more clearly the nature of the coalitions in a particular family and to begin to plan a strategy to bring such coalitions into a more functional alignment, presumably more closely approximating Example A. In Example B, for instance, the therapist might give attention to activating the marital coalition and also the coalitions between parent and offspring of the same sex and between the offspring themselves, and he might also try to attenuate to some extent the force of the existing cross-generational, cross-sexed interactions.

In general, the tactics and goals of family therapy, viewed in this light, might include making changes in the marital coalition (very commonly the case), as well as in the parent-child dyads. Although triads are not considered to any great extent in this discussion, an isolated family member, such as in Example D, might be brought into interaction with the rest of the family unit. Looking outside of the nuclear family for a moment, it would be important to consider the appropriateness of encouraging extrafamilial contacts with outside peers, both for the parents facing the "empty nest" and for growing children and adolescents. At times, when such outside interactions, especially, for example, with in-laws, seem maladaptive, modifications might have to be considered.

The therapist tries to keep the major focus on the family system and off individuals. Guilt and blame are reduced by pointing out that there are reasons why family members do what they do. The family therapist usually tries to deemphasize individual scapegoating, "sickness," and "problems." He often needs to make clear the need for mutual understanding, and to point out that everyone in the family has been doing his best, for valid reasons, although the results are not always fortunate. The healthy aspects of family functioning are supported (for example, the family can plan a weekend), whereas the "sick" or maladaptive aspects of the family functioning are counteracted (the family cannot plan a budget and is in financial difficulty).

The therapist attempts to shift the balance of relationships in the family in a more positive direction. To do this he may intervene as a mediator in family conflicts.

> In the S. family, Mr. and Mrs. S. had been married 20 years. There was a son, 17, and a daughter, 15. Mr. S. was a smooth-talking salesman who had sold his wife on how "sick" she was. His wife was a product of a family in which her mother made her feel extremely guilty because the mother's own marriage was not working. The "patient" grew up extremely masochistic, became a nurse, and had made multiple suicide attempts. In this family, the father and the two children were aligned against Mrs. S. This alignment seemed to function to cover up the father's areas of deficiency—he was not able to make a living, he was not able to set limits for the children, and so forth. Therapeutic intervention was to shift the balance of forces in the family to get more support for Mrs. S. in her attempt to resolve some of the problems that had brought them into treatment.

The therapist may first need to define and encourage expression of important issues about which the family disagrees. He resists the family's efforts to cover up conflict, and prefers to deal with recent or current issues involving available family members rather than old themes concerning absent members.[8]

He keeps the emphasis on the present and future, rather than the past. This does not mean that the past may not be usefully explored in order to deal more appropriately with the present and future. Exclusive, obsessive concentration on "spilled milk," however, usually does not lead to constructive change.

The therapist then may intervene as a mediator by, for example, emphasizing certain conflicts as being particularly important. (In general, the therapist should be in control of the process, although at times he may allow or select someone else to act as the mediator.)

In this role, he may be active, intrusive, and confronting, or he may be inactive and passive. He may point out overt conflict between two family members, or he may remain in control by refusing to take sides in a continuing dispute. He may offer an alternative viewpoint in a disagreement, or he may attack two family members in hopes of bringing a conflict to the surface.

The therapist may then side with or against any one family member, or the entire family unit, in a particular conflict. It is impossible for the therapist not to take sides, and he will always be seen by the family as doing so. The problem is, rather, for the therapist to decide under what circumstances and with whom to side as a therapeutic maneuver, and also to discover with whom the family thinks him to be siding. By judicious siding, the therapist can tip the balance in favor of more productive relating, or at least disrupt a chronic pattern of pathogenic relating.[9]

Families may attempt to resist this process of change by denying the validity or importance of the conflictual issues the therapist has emphasized, by trying to preempt the position of mediator, and by forcing the therapist into an inflexible mediator position in which he can be accused of being "unfair" (see Chapter 9).

But the therapist maintains rapport with the whole family, and must conceptualize the family as a unit. He must not consistently align himself with one or another family member and must be ready to shift support from one member or combination to another, depending on the circumstances.[10] He must know and respect each family member and must accent the positive rewards for the whole family and for each family member.[10] At the same time, he tries continually to evaluate and strengthen the marital coalition as the strongest one in a healthy family.

The family therapist may make use of advice and direction. He tries first to identify and then to change maladaptive methods of coping. Therapists often will indicate the importance of limit-setting as a method to encourage change, for example, "I think your son should begin attending school *within two weeks.*"

THE THERAPIST FUNCTIONS AS A FAMILY ROLE MODEL, EDUCATOR, AND DEMYTHOLOGIZER

On the one hand, the therapist serves as a *reality tester* for the family. He distinguishes between what is actually going on and what is fantasy. This may be in relation to behavior, attitudes, or emotions. Such reality testing is not by any means confined to grossly psychotic family members. For example, one rural family was referred for treatment when they refused to allow their children to go to school for 6 months because of the possibility of an earthquake.

On the other hand, the therapist avoids any claim to omnipotence. As much as the case allows, he helps the family do the work of changing. His intent is ultimately to enable the family to solve its own problems. The more the family can do—without the therapist—the better it will be in the long run.

The therapist serves as a *model for identification*. He can provide an education in family living, roles, clear communication, emotional honesty, problem solving, the realities of married life, and so forth. The family learns from what the therapist says and how he conducts himself. If he role-plays a more emphathic spouse to a defensive wife, the family may see the possibility for an alternative set of transactions. If the therapist is able to focus on sexual issues in an open, direct, and mature manner, he may thereby help a sexually guilt-ridden, fearful family to come to terms with these issues. The usual error is to be overly grandiose, and the therapist should be cautious about trying to remake the family in his own image.[11]

Several authors have stressed the desirability of the family therapist's being clear about his own values and concepts regarding family life. Among these is the idea of the family as a system, with both homeostatic and developmental models. The marital relationship is seen as the core of the family, with the identified patient as a signal of family distress. Family therapists usually feel that marital partners have difficulty with respect to such issues as separateness, differentness, open communication, the realities of married life, the changing phases and roles in the marriage, and the expression of healthy self-assertion. Most therapists also favor a problem-solving approach, rather than one emphasizing blame or guilt. The family therapist must clarify for himself his position on such issues as gender roles, maturity, marital roles, career, money, sex, and parental relationships to children, among other important family issues. To the extent that he is clearly aware of his own position, he stands less chance of imposing his own values and conflicts, unwittingly, in the therapy.

In marital and family therapy, the therapist often will find himself called upon to function as a *demythologizer, or philosopher of family life.* This usually involves his helping the family to experience and to make explicit covert family myths (for example, "father can't work," or "Neil is the stupid one in the family"), rather than his giving direct advice to the lovelorn or loveworn. The myths by which people live can serve as gratifying anchoring points, but some may be mutually incompatible, extreme, relatively unrealistic, or not mutually agreeable to the members of the family. In such instances these beliefs may cause disappointment and pain, and it will be part of a family therapist's job to recognize the role that they may be playing. These "myths" are discussed in greater detail in Chapter 3.

These three strategies are not necessarily mutually exclusive, and in part overlap considerably. To some extent, they represent different frames of reference for understanding and dealing with the same family phenomena. Nevertheless, each seems to offer something unique in concepts and technique. It should be clear that in a clinical situation the therapist will be hard put to remain a "purist." He will find that in his efforts to clarify communication, he may produce shifts in family coalitions, or that exploring the family's myths may lead to considerable outpouring of previously concealed affect.

These are not the only types of intervention open to the therapist, but they are the three we emphasize for the beginning therapist. There is hardly any specific technique of individual or group therapy that could not in some way or other be adapted for use in family therapy.

Some family therapists avoid the traditional techniques of individual therapy, that is, they do not concentrate on eliciting historical material, are not particularly interested in fostering increased awareness or expression of buried feelings, and do not engage in interpreting psychodynamics. They do not consider understanding and insight to be important or essential in producing change. Instead, this group of family therapists manipulates such variables as the participants and rules of therapy by active suggestion and direction. They may utilize paradoxical commands and clearly attempt to alter the arrangement and intensity of family coalitions.[12]

What is unique in family therapy is not so much the specific techniques utilized as the overall focus and strategy that aim to evaluate and produce beneficial change in the entire family system.

REFERENCES

1. Watzlawick P J, Beavin H, Jackson D D: Pragmatics of Human Communication. A Study of Interactional Patterns, Pathologies, and Paradoxes. New York, Norton, 1967.
2. Satir V: Conjoint Family Therapy: A Guide to Theory and Technique (2nd ed). Palo Alto, Ca, Science and Behavior Books, 1967.
3. Bateson G, Jackson D D, Haley J, Weakland J: Towards a theory of schizophrenia. Behav Sci 1:251–264, 1956.
4. Watzlawick P J: A review of the double bind theory. Family Process 2:132–153, 1963.
5. Scheflen A E: Stream and Structure of Communicational Behavior. Behavioral Series Monograph No. 1. Philadelphia, Eastern Pennsylvania Psychiatric Institute, 1965.
6. Ackerman N W: Treating the Troubled Family. New York, Basic Books, 1966.
7. Paul N L: The role of mourning and empathy in conjoint marital therapy, in Zuk G H, Boszormenyi-Nagy I (eds): Family Therapy and Disturbed Families. Palo Alto, Ca, Science and Behavior Books, 1967, pp 186–205.

8. Zuk G: Family Therapy: A Triadic Based Approach. New York, Behavioral Publications, 1971.
9. Zuk G: When the family therapist takes sides: A case report. Psychotherapy. 5:24–28, 1968.
10. Ackerman N W: Psychodynamics of Family Life, Diagnosis and Treatment in Family Relationships. New York, Basic Books, 1958.
11. Lefer J: Countertransference in family therapy. Journal of the Hillside Hospital 15:205–210, 1966.
12. Camp H: Structured family therapy: An outsider's perspective. Family Process 12:269–277, 1973.

8

The Course of Family Treatment

OBJECTIVES

- To become familiar with the various strategies and techniques used in the course of family treatment
- To explore some of the processes of each stage

TREATMENT STAGES

Although for clarity of presentation and thinking we have separated family evaluation and family treatment, in practice this rarely happens, nor is it particularly desirable. A process of continual evaluation takes place throughout the sessions, with the therapist constantly checking his perceptions of what is happening. At the same time, every session should have some beneficial outcome. The more skillful and experienced the therapist, the more totally is he able to blend the evaluative and therapeutic aspects and the more ready will he be to improvise variations, condensations, and extensions on some of the themes, rather than follow any one scheme rigidly in all instances. Certainly, if one is engaged in short-term crisis intervention, 30 minutes may be all that is available for evaluation. On the other hand, with no time limit for treatment, or in a training setting, one may be able to allot much more time for thorough evaluation.

Presented here are some of the possible areas of importance to be utilized by the therapist in a manner and order appropriate to the particular family. We intend to increase the range of the therapist's repertory, rather than to impose any preconceived, arbitrary framework.

A beginning therapist may want to obtain a fairly extensive history, perhaps mainly in the opening sessions, whereas a more veteran practitioner may rely on only a few bits of historical data, working more with what happens in the "here and now," and gathering longitudinal data only as needed during the course of the meetings. However, the inexperienced therapist should guard against rushing into shortcut techniques before having had the benefit of understanding in detail many different family patterns and the more standard family therapy techniques.

The therapist may decide to hear from each family member in turn on certain important issues, or he may let the verbal interaction take its own course. He may decide to call on one parent first, then the other, and then the children in descending chronological order. He may decide to call on the more easily intimidated, weaker, more passive parent (or spouse) first.

He may decide to use first names for all family members, to help put everyone on a more equal footing, or he may decide to be more formal in addressing the parents, to strengthen what may appear to him to be relatively weak generation differences and parental functioning.

He may encourage the family members to talk with each other, or he may focus the conversation largely on himself, at least at the outset or at times of stress or chaos in the sessions. (For a fuller discussion of some of these issues, see Appendix A, The Structured Family Interview.)

At the outset, the family therapist usually introduces himself and asks for the names of all family members. He then asks how he can be of help to the whole family. Usually, a statement by one of the parents of the presenting problem will follow. It usually is focused on the identified patient and is often blaming in tone. Most therapists try to get as many points of view as possible by asking other members what they think, even if they are silent.

The assumption is made that the family behavior is similar in the office to the behavior at home, although perhaps modified in some ways by the presence of the therapist. At this point, the therapist is somewhat the outsider. His main function may be to allow everyone to be heard, including the weakest members of the family. Some family members will most often be on the attack, some on the defense during the initial period. An identified patient who is an adolescent often will demand changes at home, since he is frequently the one most interested in change. An angry, frustrated spouse will demand that the marital partner change.

The therapist may point out that he will not be a decision maker for the family, but that he will try to help them clarify their problems and help them with their decision-making processes. He may act as a referee and a traffic cop when necessary, making sure that one person speaks at a time, that no one person is overwhelmed by attacks during the sessions, and that nongratifying family patterns are not allowed to continue unchallenged during the therapy sessions. He creates an atmosphere that will encourage the verbal expression of feelings toward constructive ends.

He makes it clear that he understands that in an unhappy family everyone "hurts," and that everyone wants to get something positive out of the sessions. He conveys that everyone in the family is doing the best he or she can, and that one needs to understand the motives of oneself and of others, and that it happens in life that attitudes and actions that are well intentioned nevertheless sometimes are less than totally positive in their outcomes.

Families vary considerably in their readiness to move from the discussion of the current crisis situation to an exploration of the family's patterns and history. We follow the family's lead in these respects. Thus, for example, a therapist may be willing to start the sessions even though the father is absent, and may sense that the family members need some time to talk about the "badness" of one of the offspring. It is important that the therapist himself get an idea of what the family's mode of operations is in this respect, and that he communicate a sense of respect for and understanding of the family's initial point of view. At the same time he will need to guard against being so passive and accepting that nothing new has been added to the equation. The family's experience in the therapy hour should not be merely a repetition of the nongratifying interactional patterns for which they originally sought help. It may be opportune to indicate to the family that individual problems often are related to family problems and to state that it may be helpful to all concerned to find out more about the family as a whole, so as to enable each member and the family as an entity to benefit from the treatment.

It may be desirable to move on to a longitudinal, chronological narrative of the family's history (perhaps through three generations) or instead to begin with a cross-sectional inventory of how the family currently functions. Which of these areas is elucidated first will depend on the therapist's predilections, the family's distress, and the nature of the difficulty. The main longitudinal data that might be gathered refer to the period of courtship, engagement, marriage, honeymoon, early years of marriage prior to the arrival of children, and the changes in the family as a result of the first child and each subsequent child.

One may start with the courtship period (which is, in part, predictive of marital patterns), move on to marriage, and then work backward, with each partner going back to his or her original family. For each partner, one can discuss the history prior to the marriage, including any previous marriages. In going back to the parents' families of origin, it is important to get a picture of the functioning of those families to serve as groundwork for understanding the present family and its problems. Careful attention must be given not only to recollections of the past and to expressions regarding attitudes and values, but also to overt behavior. For example, gross difficulties in sexual adjustment should be carefully delineated by taking a thorough and complete sexual history. This is something that, in our experience, still is done all too rarely in the field of family therapy, as though sexual problems were regarded as only secondary to other interpersonal difficulties.

However, primary difficulties in sexual adjustment will often sour the rest of the marital relationship. Sometimes sexual difficulties were the first major area of difficulty in the marital union, or have proven to be the difficulty of preeminent concern to the married couple, and perhaps the one most difficult for them to deal with. There are couples who appear to need and who will benefit from specific therapy directed toward bettering their sexual adjustment, and to the extent that this can be done satisfactorily, other areas of marital and family interaction may then markedly improve. The point, therefore, is to evaluate the sexual adjustment of the marital pair at least as carefully as other areas of marital and family interaction. It is not safe to assume that any sexual problems are secondary and will resolve themselves more or less spontaneously, if only other areas of family difficulty are improved.[1]

Another area often overlooked or slighted in the evaluation phase is the family's dealings with money. We have found this to be an important arena of marital and family friction. As with sexuality, this issue is not always merely secondary to other marital problems. Some marital couples have simply never been able to work out a satisfactory way of managing money as a marital pair. It certainly is also the case that any other sort of marital problem may be reflected in fights about money, just as they may be reflected in sexual maladjustment.

The amount and type of data to be assembled will be strongly influenced by the current phase of the family life cycle. Often, it seems that families seek help in relation to developmental crises in the normal family life cycle. Therefore, it would be appropriate to concentrate on material relevant to issues pertaining to that particular phase of family life. It would then make a difference if one were dealing with a couple in the first year of marriage or a family whose last offspring is preparing to leave home; the relative emphasis, as well as some of the specific content of the history to be gathered, would be quite different.

Should the family present the history or should the therapist structure the history with an outline? Most therapists seem to combine both approaches. This is because the family knows itself, in some ways better than the therapist. It is often helpful, therefore, to let the family members talk until they run "dry." On the other hand, the therapist presumably has expertise in helping families with problems and can help them in structuring a history. What is excluded by the structuring usually will emerge as time goes on, but what is "missed" by not structuring (for example, not taking a sexual history) may never be revealed.

History gathering requires complex skills. Excellent references on methodology for getting a family history include works by Satir,[2] Bell,[3] and the Group for the Advancement of Psychiatry.[4] There are also training films on family therapy, parts of which demonstrate history taking.[5-8]

Summary of Treatment Stages

Early stage. This chapter has offered a brief discussion of the early and middle stages of treatment. Some of the primary concerns of the early stage include

1. Detailing the primary problems
2. Clarifying the goals for treatment
3. Solidifying the therapeutic contract
4. Strengthening the therapeutic relationship
5. Shifting the focus from one member to the family
6. Decreasing guilt and blame
7. Pointing out that different family members have different views of what is going on, so as to get each member to empathize with the others

During this phase, the therapist comes to a better understanding of the life of the family, making contact and promoting empathy and communication. Some major nonproductive conflicts are exposed and scapegoating is neutralized. When a child is the identified patient, there begins a painful shift to focus away from the child and onto the parents.

Middle stage. What the therapist does in this stage will vary, depending on the areas that have been singled out as of primary importance and the goals that have been established. Most commonly, examples of persistent interpersonal patterns and attitudes, preferably drawn from recent or "here and now" interactions, are discussed repeatedly. Old nonfunctional coalitions, rules, myths, and role models are challenged, and the possibility of alternative modes is presented. New habits of thinking, feeling, and interacting take time to develop, and much repetition is often required. At the same time, resistance to change comes to the fore, and must be dealt with accordingly (see Chapter 9).

The initial focus may be on the identified patient, then move to the family. Often, the identified patient may improve before the family does.

End stage. In the closing phase, the therapist reviews with the family which goals have been achieved and which have not. It is often useful to review the entire course of therapy, including the original problems and goals. Another prime task is to lay a foundation for solving future conflicts. It is important to acknowledge that some behavior cannot be changed and that life will continue to be filled with problems. Videotape playback may be helpful here, so that the family can see what it looked like at the start of treatment, compared to the present.

The question often arises, how do you know when to stop therapy? In answering this, the importance of setting goals becomes obvious. If the goals are achieved, you can stop. If the goals are not achieved, but have been worked out to the extent of the capabilities of therapist and family, therapy should stop. If the treatment has been successful, the therapist often will note new coping patterns established, a sense of relative calm in the family (compared to the onset of therapy), and a sense of empathy by family members for each other. Often, together with these factors will come a recognition that the family itself seems capable of dealing satisfactorily with new situations as they arise, and at the same time there will seem to be little to talk about in the sessions and little sense of urgency. Nonproductive quarreling and conflict having been reduced, the family is freer to disagree openly and has methods of living with and working out its differences and separateness. The family seems less inflexible in its rules and organization, and appears more able to grow and develop. Individual family members are symptomatically improved, and positive channels of interaction are available between all family members. There is improved agreement about family roles and functions.

During this phase, there may be an exacerbation of presenting symptoms. For example, the son may begin hallucinating again because the father has stopped communicating with the mother. This is usually short-lived. Clinical experience suggests that it represents a temporary response to the anxiety of terminating treatment, rather than a treatment failure. It is thus part of the "separation" process.

SPECIFIC TECHNIQUES AND CONSIDERATIONS

During the course of treatment, other techniques in addition to those described in Chapter 7 can be employed, depending on the specific case or situation. Most of these techniques are newer, interesting, innovative, have their strong proponents, and are mentioned here for the sake of completeness.

1. Family sculpture. This is a technique[9] in which the therapist asks all the members of the family to create a physical representation of their relationships at one point in time by arranging their bodies in space. For example, if the mother feels oppressed, the family members may arrange themselves with the father standing on top of the mother. The technique can be used as part of the diagnostic workup to generate hypotheses or to represent concretely a concept being worked on during the course of therapy. Both the content of the sculpture and the way the sculptor uses mass and form are examined.

2. Multiple family group therapy.[10-10c] This bears somewhat the relationship to conjoint family therapy that group therapy bears to individual treatment. Several family units meet together for therapy sessions; the size of such groups has varied from 3 to 30 families, with one or more therapists. Also, weekend family marathons[11] have been reported, in which one or several entire family units get together for extended periods (anywhere from 8 to 12 hours or longer) with leaders (or "facilitators") for a variety of intensive types of encounters, usually including affect catharsis and nonverbal experiencing.

3. Videotape. The ready availability of video equipment has made possible its increasing use. Therapists often find it profitable to review their sessions and to have a record of an entire course of therapy. Immediate playback of a videotape helps families attain some psychological distance, makes them increasingly self-aware, helps to correct distortions or conflicts about communication, and is invaluable in revealing the important nonverbal aspects of interactions that might otherwise be lost.[12] Families often comment constructively on their own videotaped interactions in a way they might not readily accept from a therapist.[7]

4. Audiotape. This has also been used as an adjunct to family therapy.[13] A tape of the session can be made and the family can take it home and listen to it. Or, a tape can be made at home and then played in the session.

5. Family tasks. Family therapy focuses on behavioral change. Accordingly, many family therapists routinely "prescribe" various tasks for the family to perform during the session and between sessions. The rationale is for the family to practice behavior patterns outside the session, for the therapist (rather than the family) to control the symptom or problem, thus moving it out of the control and power structure of the family, and to help realign coalitions. For example, a family that has not had any recreational activity together in several years may be asked to take a vacation

together, or a husband and wife are instructed to discuss a "family secret" (see Appendix A). The danger in such an approach lies in asking the family to do something they are incapable of or not ready for (presumably timing of the task is an important issue). Such techniques have been criticized by therapists with a strong orientation to verbal techniques as "superficial and not getting to the root of things." The correctness of either the technique or the criticism is unclear at this time.

Minuchin[14] has described, especially when working with disorganized lower class ghetto families, assigning someone in the family to perform some specific task important to the family. Such tasks might involve getting the family registered with a housing agency or helping it in some other way to cope with the realities of its basic needs. This serves to train and strengthen the family unit's ability to handle its problems in concrete terms, and helps to solidify the often shaky and inadequate manner in which the family carries out its basic tasks and provides for its elemental needs. It can give such a family the experience of being able to accomplish something meaningful to it in its daily struggle for existence and stability, better than would the more symbolic, attitudinal, psychological process that may be appropriate for middle and upper class families.

6. Prescribing the symptoms. Both Jackson and Haley[15] have written about a therapeutic technique in which the therapist "prescribes the symptoms." Whereas the symptoms previously may have seemed out of anyone's control, after the therapist "orders" the family members (or individual) to continue and perhaps increase the symptoms, they begin to lose their autonomy, mystery, and power. They appear to come under the therapist's control, the participants in the behavior become more conscious of them, and often the behavior lessens or disappears. A marital couple that has engaged in nonproductive arguing now finds that the therapist has asked them to continue fighting and to increase it; the couple is told to fight about the menu before dinner so that they can enjoy the food. This injunction jars the continuing process, and they may rebel against the outsider's orders.

7. Network therapy. Speck[16,17] has described this new approach to the problem of the identified patient. All members of the kinship system, all friends of the family and "significant others" (some 30 to 40 people) are brought together to work on the problem. This technique includes all persons who bear on the problem, thus obviating such resistances to change as "the absent member," the family friend, and so forth, and adding "healthier" voices to the problem.

8. Psychodrama and role-playing. These techniques have also been

used to help families play out family problems and work out new patterns. They are especially useful in nonverbal families.[18] Role reversal is especially useful for developing empathy in family members.

9. Gestalt therapy. In treating family problems, the therapist stresses that the only real time is the present (instead of rehashing the past), each individual is responsible for his or her own behavior (this counters the familiar resistance, "I did it only because he or she made me do it"), and symptoms and conflicts are the here and now expressions of unfinished situations of childhood which can be finished in treatment.[19]

10. Working with poverty families. Special modifications of family therapy have been suggested for the needs of poor families. A meaningful balance must be struck between dealing with reality issues (food, clothing, and so forth) and family psychological issues. Too often, the former areas have been neglected, and the technique is to utilize such events as housing problems or food shortage as a way into the affective, communicational, and structural aspects of the family.[18,20,21]

Hours of agencies and therapists must be more flexible than they have been in the past. There should be an emphasis on concrete activities (rather than insight and intellectual pronouncement), current issues (rather than past), and concrete reality (rather than fantasies) from session to session. The therapist often will have to go to the family rather than they to him. The therapist thus goes into the community, and in this context family psychiatry serves as a basis for community psychiatry.

11. Working with wealthy families. Many upper socioeconomic class families will be found to be quite different, in many respects, from middle or lower socioeconomic class families. Marital coalitions may be much less well-structured than in middle socioeconomic class families, and there may be a considerable lack of emotional cohesiveness that is oddly reminiscent of the lower socioeconomic class family. Parenting may be intermittent, inconsistent, and largely managed by people other than the parents, again similar to the pattern in some low income families. Offspring in these families may evidence an inability to formulate life goals and may seem to drift aimlessly. A family therapist for such families must be sensitive to the particular patterns found in them, including their tendency to "escape" from difficulties through the use of money, and their ability to "bribe" the therapist with high fees and then to treat him more like a servant.

12. Working with the one-parent family. One-parent families may be

brought about by parental separation or divorce, or by the death of one spouse. The family therapist will, of course, be sensitive to the impact of such developments, both in the short range and over a longer period of time. Such evaluation of the impact of an absent spouse on the remaining family unit must take into account the phase of family development in which the absence occurred, as well as its total length, the feelings of the remaining family members about the nonpresent member, and the mechanisms the family has utilized in coping with its unusual constellation. For example, for the remaining spouse, the absence of a partner can lead to loneliness and the increased burden of not being able to share in marital and parental role complementarity. The remaining spouse may have to be both mother and father for the children.

These situations are often difficult ones for the therapist to deal with, and no pat answers seem to be available. A clarification of feelings about the loss may be helpful, as well as a realistic assessment of the demands and possibilites in the current family configuration. Where appropriate, external help in the form of re-placement parental role models, extended family, and other community resources, such as social agencies, have been encouraged.

13. Brief and crisis intervention treatment. Some therapists utilize "brief" or "crisis intervention" family therapy, distinguished, presumably, from "long-term" or "noncrisis" treatment. The elements of a brief therapy "set" important for success in this type of treatment are

> therapist motivation for brief therapy, the "therapeutic pressure" of time-limited therapy and the expectation of improvement, the collaborative effort of therapist and family in defining a focus in therapy and working toward specific treatment goals, rapid development of the therapeutic alliance, termination as an issue from the onset of therapy, a family-oriented approach in therapy, the active definition and utilization of the family's strengths in coping with their difficulties, and encouraging the family to return for further consultation if additional stress or crises arise (p. 48).[22]

Although some theorists indicate that at times of crisis families and individuals may be most responsive to trying out new patterns, others feel that, especially in very severe disturbances, the wiser course is to attempt first to restabilize the family along preexisting, familiar lines. Only after the fire has been put out can there be any thought of rebuilding the house. The therapist would be even more directive and supportive than usual, and attempt to enlist any individuals or other resources outside the family who might be of assistance.

14. The family and genetic counseling. Concurrent with the rapid explosion in knowledge about genetic diseases, there has been a great need for genetic counseling. The primary task of genetic counseling is to determine the effect of the presumed medical problem, or "bad genes," or the "defective" baby on the family's relationship. To do this, one must first assess the prior family relationship and then use this information to counsel in a way that will maximally increase the family's chances of successful functioning. Most commonly, parents tend to blame each other for the difficulty. This causes an increased emotional burden to both parents and to the expected child.

It is the common experience of genetic counselors to find that families "forget" a great deal of the information they have been given in counseling. This is especially true when a member's self-esteem is low. It is likely that family members use the genetic information they are given in the service of the family's emotional needs, and rather than being forgotten, it is repressed, denied, distorted, magnified, to fit the family's needs. For example, the mother has been angry with the father. She may use the information of genetic defect as "proof" of the father's defects. The alert genetic counselor must be aware of this and treat accordingly. Guilt and blame should be kept to a minimum, and better patterns of coping for the family must be explored. If brief, time-limited counseling is not effective, then referral for family therapy may be indicated.

REFERENCES

1. Masters W, Johnson V: Human Sexual Response. Boston, Little, Brown, 1966.
2. Satir V: Conjoint Family Therapy: A Guide to Theory and Technique (ed 2). Palo Alto, Ca, Science and Behavior Books, 1967.
3. Bell J E: Family Group Therapy. Public Health Monograph No. 64. Washington, D. C, Department of Health, Education and Welfare, Public Health Service, 1961.
4. Group for the Advancement of Psychiatry. The Case History Method in the Study of Family Process. Report No. 76. New York, Group for the Advancement of Psychiatry, 1970.
5. The Enemy and Myself. 16 mm black and white sound film, 50 min., by Nathan Ackerman, M.D. (The Family Institute, New York, N Y 10021).
6. Family in Crisis. 16 mm color sound film, 48 min., by David R. Kessler, M.D. (Langley Porter Neuropsychiatric Institute, University of California San Francisco Medical Center, San Francisco, Ca 94143.

7. Family Therapy: An Introduction. 16 mm black and white sound film, 43 min., by Ira D. Glick, M.D. (University of California Medical Center, San Francisco, Ca 94143) and George J. Marshall, Sr.

8. In and Out of Psychosis: A Family Study. 16 mm black and white sound film, 120 min., by Nathan Ackerman, M.D. (The Family Institute, New York, NY 10021).

9. Simon R: Sculpting the family. Family Process 11:49–58, 1972.

10. Blinder M, Colman A, Curry A, Kessler D: "MCFT": Simultaneous treatment of several families. Am J Psychotherapy 19:559–569, 1965.

10a. Laqueur H P: Multiple family therapy and general systems theory, in Ackerman N W (ed): Family Therapy in Transition. Boston, Little, Brown, 1970, pp 82–93.

10b. Curry A: Therapeutic management of a multiple family group. International Journal of Group Psychotherapy, 15:90–96, 1965.

10c. Laqueur P, Wells C, Agresti M: Multiple-family therapy in a state hospital. Hospital and Community Psychiatry 20:13–20, 1969.

11. Landes J, Winter W: A new strategy for treating disintegrating families. Family Process 5:1–20, 1966.

12. Silk S: The use of videotape in brief joint marital therapy. Am J Psychotherapy 26:417–424, 1972.

13. David A: Using audiotape as an adjunct to family therapy: Three case reports. Psychotherapy 7:28–32, 1970.

14. Minuchin S, Montalvo B, Guerney B G, Rosman B L, Shumer F: Families of the Slums: An Exploration of Their Structure and Treatment. New York, Basic Books, 1967.

15. Haley J: Strategies of Psychotherapy. New York, Grune & Stratton, 1963.

16. Speck R V, Rueveni U: Network therapy: A developing concept. Family Process 8:182–191, 1969.

17. Speck R V, Attneave C: Network therapy, in Haley J (ed): Changing Families. New York, Grune & Stratton, 1971, pp 312–332.

18. McKinney J: Adapting family therapy to multi-deficit families. Social Casework 51:237–333, 1970.

19. Leveton A: Elizabeth is frightened. Voices 8:4–13, 1972.

20. Mannino F, Shore M: Ecologically oriented family interaction. Family Process 11:499–504, 1972.

21. Adams P: Functions of the lower-class partial family. Am J Psychiatry 130:200–203, 1973.

22. Rosenthal A, Levine S: Brief psychotherapy with children: Process of therapy, in Barten B H, Barten S S (eds): Children and Their Parents in Brief Therapy. New York, Behavioral Publications, 1973, pp. 40–48.

9

Family Treatment: Resistance to Change

OBJECTIVES

- To list and understand resistances to change in the family
- To consider strategies to counteract these resistances and promote change in the family
- To understand therapist reactions to the family that interfere with progress in the family

DEFINITION

Since in family therapy the primary focus is on change, patterns and transactions that prevent change can be thought of as possible resistances. These would include the withholding of pertinent material; individual behavior, such as missing sessions; and interactional behavior, such as maintaining the focus on the scapegoat, talking at the same time as everyone else, attempting to change the conditions of the contract (schedule of sessions, and so forth), and blaming the therapist for being unfair and for taking sides.

TYPES OF FAMILY RESISTANCE

Solomon[1] has compiled an extensive list of family resistances. He enumerates them as follows:

A) *Resistances to Therapy*

    1) Silence, passivity, superficial discussion or intellectualization, used to avoid emotional involvement.

    2) Demanding practical advice or counselling to avoid dealing with conflict.

    3) Denial of the therapist's clarifications, confrontations or interpretations.

    4) Denial of previously expressed awareness or insight.

    5) Denial of the therapist's ability to understand the problem on the basis of ethnic, linguistic or other cultural differences.

    6) Fatalistic attitude in which one accepts blame and indicates inability to change.

    7) Denial of ability to pay for treatment.

    8) Miraculous loss of symptoms or, conversely, aggravation of symptoms used as a ploy to terminate therapy.

    9) Coming to sessions late and/or avoidance of sessions.

    10) Drop-out—unilateral termination of therapy by the family.

B) *Resistance to Interaction*

    1) Refusal (usually by parents) to bring up new or meaningful material while exhorting the others to do so.

    2) Asking other family members questions to avoid self-involvement in meaningful interaction.

    3) Diversion, distraction, interruption or other means of changing an emotionally charged subject.

    4) Refusal to communicate in front of other family member(s).

    5) Using a second language to exclude another member from the interaction.

    6) Absent Member Manoeuver—talking about an absent member to avoid dealing with current interaction.

C) *Family Specific Resistances*

    1) Varied manoeuvers to avoid dealing with the marital conflict.

    2) Scapegoating—insistence that the presenting patient is the main or only family problem; offering oneself as a scapegoat, or picking on the scapegoat to avoid anxiety-laden interaction.

    3) Prediction of persistence of the presenting symptoms or of the impossibility of change.

    4) Denial of evident change in role behaviour or of improvement in the presenting patient.

    5) Denial of evident affect expressed by another family member.

    6) Protecting or defending another member so that he will persist in maintaining his behavior and resist change.

    7) Family Secrets—a family consensus to withhold certain meaningful information from the therapist.

8) Injunctions against family disloyalty to prevent the uncovering of conflict.
9) Threatening to desert the family as change approaches.
10) Threatening to abandon a family member who effects change.
11) Using other family members as an excuse to avoid therapy (pp. 22–23).

The reasons for resistance include the family's fear of change, at the same time that they want relief of their acute distress. The family is often reluctant to change because, even if the old system was bad, it was familiar; change involves giving up old, familiar patterns. Furthermore, as bad as they were, these old patterns may be better than anything else the family can conceive of.[2]

In addition, families may anticipate that getting involved in therapy may not improve their situation, and that no real change can be expected. They may even fear that therapy will make their lot worse, through exposure of their real feelings, with resulting anger and recriminations. They often feel that it may be better to "let sleeping dogs lie." Too much exploration might lead ultimately to the break-up of the marital or family unit, an outcome which the symptoms may in some way have been attempting to prevent. Someone may go "crazy" if treatment goes too far or, at least, people in the family will feel worse (for example, guiltier) as a result. These are some of the prominent factors underlying specific resistance maneuvers.

Hidden resistance can account for lack of improvement in a family that otherwise seems to have good overt motivation. The family resistances shift back and forth, and their intensity may vary with the content of the sessions. It may be important to recognize that the patient himself is not wholly a "victim." He, too, controls by means of his own resistances. Resistance shifts from one member to another, depending upon content. A mother, for example, may want to talk about the father's drinking, but may balk at discussing her own inability to clean up the house or go to work. A father may stay away from therapy, leaving the mother and identified patient together.

There is often a massive resistance in the middle phase of treatment, because the immediate crisis of the identified patient is past and the family is not hurting so much.

A few of the many specific types of resistance will now be discussed in somewhat greater detail.

Family Secrets

Individuals in the family often have "secrets" that, in most cases, are known but not acknowledged by other family members. These may involve actual overt behavior, such as marital infidelity, that one marital partner feels he has been able to conceal from the other, or thoughts, feelings, and attitudes that family members believe others are not aware of, for example, when parents do not realize that children pick up the general emotional tone existing between mother and father.

More often than not, in our experience, helping the family bring out into the open these pseudosecrets results in a clearing of the general artifical atmosphere and eventually, if not immediately, a sense of relief and greater mutual understanding. The therapist should, however, be prepared to deal with acute shock waves (or pseudoshock waves) at the time the "secret" first emerges. When an individual in a family requests an individual session to reveal a "secret," most therapists listen and try to encourage him to bring up the "secret" within the family setting if it is important to the therapy. If, for example, one of the spouses has an incurable illness and the other spouse does not know about it, the reasons and need for the secrecy would be explored. If the "secret" does not seem crucial, some therapists would argue "let sleeping dogs lie." Less commonly, a family member may insist on "total honesty" as a way of hurting another family member. For example, a parent might report to a child every negative feeling that crosses his or her mind, in the guise of "honesty."

Not only should it be clear that family work takes precedence over individual work, the therapist must also guard against being entrapped and potentially "blackmailed" by becoming a "secrets-bearer." However, exploration of the parental relationship, including sexual behavior, is often best done without the children present. Therefore, most family therapists spend at least some time with the marital couple alone. With many types of material, it is commonly the children who let the cat out of the bag and reveal overtly what was thought by others to be secret.

Absent Member

In general, the therapist should try to ensure that each family member sees the positive value for himself (as well as for other family members) to be derived from attending the sessions. If necessary, the therapist can start with the focus on the identified patient ("We're only here to help Junior; there are no other problems in the family.").

When a family member is consistently missing from the sessions, he is assumed to be absent not only because he does not want to come, but because of some overt, or, more often, covert, agreement on the part of the family that he not attend. In trying to deal with this type of resistance, the easiest course is first to note explicitly the absence of a member. Often, merely noting the absence does prove effective. If this intervention does not work, then reasons for the absence (job, anger, and so forth) are explored. Later, interpretation may be indicated ("Perhaps you don't want Dad to come in"). At any point, the therapist should not hesitate to contact the family member and clarify the reasons for nonattendance. A direct message from the therapist usually carries a different implication from one that comes from the family. In this way the therapist at least will be certain that the family member has received the message, which will often be perceived as much more positive in tone and less negatively contaminated emotionally than one that is conveyed by the family.

One way that has been found to be effective in getting the whole family involved in therapy is to have the early sessions in the home. This technique is especially useful for resistant fathers or other family members who do not want to come to the therapist's office.

Finally, it may be necessary and desirable to discuss the limitations on what can be accomplished if only the incomplete family is seen in treatment. The decision will have to be arrived at as to whether to continue therapy under these circumstances or to terminate. In some cases, one member will absolutely refuse treatment, and seeing the rest of the family may be preferable to not seeing the family at all.

The Family Friend

At times it may become clear that a "significant other" person (such as a friend, lawyer, other physician) is strongly influencing the family in directions contrary to those of therapy. This resistance is much more common than suspected and of itself can often account for lack of change. Therapeutic management often consists of bringing in the friend. This course must be weighed against the disadvantages discussed in Chapter 7 about participants, but as a short-term technique it is often helpful. Exploring in detail the friend's influence, and how it is being used by the family, even with the friend absent, may sometimes prove fruitful.

Sexual Material

Family members may not discuss sexual material because "the children are present." Actually, the children usually know many of the intimate sexual details of the family, certainly at least in terms of the emotional climate existing between the marital pair. This may sound surprising, but it has been true in our experience. However, sexual material can often be discussed in general terms, for example, closeness between parents, followed by separate sessions, as indicated, for the parents alone to discuss more intimate material.

FAMILY REACTIONS TO THE THERAPIST

The therapist will be the recipient of a combination of feelings, attitudes, and behaviors from each of the family members. These may be positive or negative in tone. They may be relatively appropriate and productive to the therapy situation. However, to the extent that they are inappropriate and nonproductive, they may be based on a carryover from problematic important past relationships. The therapist must be alert to such phenomena and will need to deal especially with those very strongly positive or negative relationship factors in the treatment that appear to be getting in the way.

The following are some common types of reactions to the therapist: he can be viewed as judge ("You decide who's right and who's wrong"), as a focus of all anger ("If it weren't for you we'd be OK"), as a curing figure ("You'll fix us up, Doctor. We don't have to discuss our problems"), as an intruder ("If you didn't ask all kinds of questions, we'd be OK"), and as a rejector ("If you weren't against us, we'd have no problems").

A traditional method for handling such issues is to call attention to the phenomenon, clarify the unspoken communication involved, explore the degree of appropriateness to the present situation, and delineate the historical background and development of such reactions and their specific correlations with other current happenings in the family situation and in the therapy. Such reactions may be put to good use in treatment by helping to clarify the usual kinds of important nonproductive interactions that occur, and indicating the way toward more productive processes. Thus, resistances may represent core interpersonal issues in microcosm, and are often utilized in important ways by experienced therapists.

THERAPIST REACTIONS TO THE FAMILY

The therapist, too, may develop unrealistic and inappropriate reactions, and these likewise may be of such intensity and nature as to present difficulties in treatment. When this occurs, the therapist will have to be able to recognize and deal with the situation. For example, the therapist may act toward the patient and family as though they were the therapist's own family, both past and present.

In individual therapy there is a one-to-one therapist-to-patient relationship. In the family therapy setting the relationship is quite different. The therapist can act out his feelings with any member of the family.

As in individual therapy, the therapist must avoid being drawn into a role that confirms the reality of the patient's misconceptions. The therapist's attitudes to such matters as family, marriage, and money, for example, must be open to his/her introspection and worked through so as not to interfere with the therapy.

In the early phase of treatment, the therapist may try to totally to remake the family. There may be much blaming. In the middle phase of treatment he may become overly identified with various family members. In the late phases he may have difficulty in separating.[3]

Certain psychiatric syndromes lend themselves to particular inappropriate reactions by the therapist. Specifically, in families with a member who has schizophrenia, the mother may be the therapist's target, whereas in families with a delinquent member, the target may be the father.

In family therapy, in contrast to individual therapy, the presence of more members helps to keep a better check on the therapist's reactions. That is, families do not hesitate to point out to the therapist if he is reacting inappropriately to a family member. Another such check is the presence of a cotherapist.

Management of such difficulties involves, first of all, the therapist's being aware of "conflict areas" in himself. He should also be aware of his own value system (see Chapter 7). Having undergone therapy himself may be of help, and this includes both individual psychotherapy and, especially, family therapy. Supervision during training is mandatory, and may be beneficial even afterward. The therapist should remember that his views are not universally applicable, and he should support individual family member's solutions as long as they are helpful.

REFERENCES

1. Solomon M: Family therapy dropouts: Resistance to change. Canadian Psychiatric Association Journal, 14:21–29, 1969.
2. Greenberg I M, Glick I D, Match S, Riback S S: Family therapy: Indications and rationale. Arch Gen Psychiatry 10:7–25, 1964.
3. Whitaker C, Felder R E, Warkentin J: Countertransference in the family treatment of schizophrenia, in Boszormenyi-Nagy I, Framo J L (eds): Intensive Family Therapy. New York, Harper and Row, 1965, pp 323–342.

10

Indications and Contraindications for Family Treatment

OBJECTIVES

- To understand the general and specific indications for family treatment, including those instances where there is an identified patient
- To recognize the contraindications for family treatment
- To appreciate other factors that bear on indications and contraindications

Some family therapists feel that their field offers the best hope for many types of interpersonal distress. They tend to feel that it should be the exclusive method to be used, and not be mixed with others, for example, with individual psychotherapy and psychopharmacology. Other therapists, however, utilize family therapy as only one type among many, but feel that it is "not a panacea, a substitute for all other approaches, or even appropriate in all cases as a total self-contained service" (p. 543).[1]

INDICATIONS

In general, family treatment is indicated when either the therapist conceptualizes and/or the family indicates that the family system is involved to a significant or a major degree in some type of psychosocial problem. Family treatment is appropriate for those situations in which the family's ability to perform its basic functions is inadequate. These func-tions have been discussed in Chapters 2 and 3.

Family treatment has been recommended for all stages of the family life cycle, for "identified patients" (or clients) with all types of difficulty (psychiatric, correctional,[2] medical,[3,4,5] educational, and so forth), or for situations in which there are obvious conflicts between a family member and the community.

For example, marital conflict and dissatisfaction seem to lend them-selves especially well to conjoint marital treatment. Yet, it is surprising and somewhat dismaying to see how often such problems still are dealt with on an individual basis, with perhaps only one of the marital partners in treatment, with relatively little or no attention paid to the impact of the individual treatment on the marital system and the marital partner. The field of marital counseling[6,7,8] (and common sense) has long since indi-cated the need to see the marital couple together in such instances, and this trend appears to be growing. Many authors believe it is more efficient in both time and cost to treat a whole family rather than an individual family member (that is, the identified patient). A further advantage of family therapy is that the role of the identified patient in multiproblem families often shifts from one member to another, so that in the long run family therapy is more efficacious.

In recent years, conjoint treatment for sexual problems has shown increasing promise, especially with the work of Masters and Johnson[9] and their colleagues. Common sexual problems have often been very difficult to ameliorate when treated on an individual basis. When these same problems are viewed in an interactional framework and treated with both partners present—using a combination of sex therapy and marital therapy—surprisingly effective results have been obtained. This ap-proach is just one example of the value of conjoint treatment in marital problems.

When a child is the identified patient, it has long been the practice in child guidance clinics to involve at least one of the parents, usually in collateral treatment in which patient and parent are both in individual treatment but with different therapists. This represents at least token recognition of the importance of the family in the difficulty and in its resolution.

A much more thorough-going approach than this, however, seems indicated in these cases, with evaluation of the possible role of the child as the "symptom bearer" of more general family problems, often unre-solved marital issues. It is not unusual in such situations for the marital partners to be seen as a couple for a major part of the treatment. The "identified patient" may benefit from some individual attention addressed to his or her particular symptoms and psychosocial difficulties. A common sequence of events is for the entire family to start out in treatment together, and for various individual dyads and triads to be separated out for special attention after an interval. Of these, the marital dyad is unquestionably the most important. Some family therapists would go even further, suggesting that wherever there is a symptomatic child before puberty, family treatment is indicated, unless there are specific contraindications.

With the adolescent as the "identified patient," focus on the family is still indicated, especially while the adolescent is living at home, having not yet established psychological and financial autonomy. In treating a family with an adolescent "authority problem," inclusion of the entire family group can dilute the adolescent's feelings about the therapist. In these instances, too, a good deal of attention must often be focused on the marital partnership, and the adolescent will often be found to benefit from individual attention as well as the encouragement of peer group relationships. Presumably, the more emancipated the adolescent, the less will be the need for conjoint family sessions, and the more the emphasis can be placed on individual and/or peer group sessions.

Other intimate interpersonal systems, less formally organized and recognized than marriages and families, may lend themselves successfully to conjoint interventions. Couples who are involved significantly with one another, whether or not they are married and living together, or are heterosexual or homosexual dyads, have been effectively treated.

Even when the guidelines enumerated above are recognized, the question nevertheless sometimes arises as to when to opt for family treatment rather than for individual, group, or other modalities. It should be noted that an individual's psychological sensitivity or "insight" into his problem is not a necessary prerequisite for his benefiting from family treatment. Change in families as well as in individuals can and often does occur without "insight." A further advantage is that the problem can be discussed with the relevant persons participating, so it is not necessary to rely on one person's point of view. The marital or family system may be the treatment of choice when:

1. *It is thought that the identified patient has symptomatology that is the manifestation of a disturbed family as a whole.* This is a basic premise of family therapy, that is, that the individual in distress may be symptom bearer for a disturbed family unit. The reader is again referred to Chapters 2 and 3.

2. *There is no improvement with individual therapy.* Family evaluation often can explain why there has been no improvement in such cases. The therapist may recognize only later that the lack of improvement may have had to do with marital or family factors that have been

overlooked. Enlarging the conceptual field to include the family and actually bringing the family into the treatment session often helps to break such deadlocks. For example, if the mother and father are having trouble communicating, they would be unable to work effectively together in setting limits on the delinquent behavior of the son, who is the identified patient. Or, the family environment may prevent the individual from benefiting in individual therapy because he is pulled in opposite directions by warring factions in the family.[10] For instance, a father wants the son to work but the mother wants to keep the son home with her.

3. *As a result of therapy with one member, stress or symptoms develop in other family members.* On occasion there may be successful treatment of one family member, but concomitantly another family member becomes symptomatic. Upon examination, one sees that factors of family equilibrium and homeostasis may not have been taken fully into account, and at such points other family members should be brought into the treatment arena.

   For example, the secondary gain of illness may be great for one or more members of the family.[10] If a mother is unable to function and psychologically needs to take care of her son who will not go to school, it will be difficult to get the son back to school; were this effort successful without the mother's involvement, a major increase in her symptomatology would likely occur.

4. *The individual patient seems unable to utilize the intrapsychic, interpretive mode of some forms of individual treatment, and/or uses most of the therapy sessions to talk about a family member.* A relatively common situation of this sort is that in which one marital partner comes into treatment ostensibly to complain about the spouse or to get the spouse into treatment. The marital therapist is often able, by skillful rechanneling of the underlying needs and concerns, to get both partners involved in a joint endeavor to examine their marital interaction. He may do this by reconceptualizing the problem from the individual to the marital–interactive sphere by asking both parties to participate, helping both clarify what they stand to gain by therapy.

5. *The identified patient is in a hospital or other institutional setting.* It has been found empirically that improvement occurring during the course of institutionalization often becomes totally negated when the family member returns to his family, if family members have only been involved in last minute discharge planning.

   A patient may be hospitalized with perhaps one goal being to remove him from the supposedly psychonoxious family environment. When the hospitalized patient becomes asymptomatic, attempts at hospital discharge may be made. At such times, if continuing work has not gone on with the family, one of several undesirable outcomes may result. The recovered patient will return to the same family setting, only soon again to become symptomatic. Or, the recovered patient finds that the family has "closed ranks" in his absence, and there no longer appears to be any psychological room for him in the family. Or, plans may be made for the recovered patient to leave the hospital but live away from his family. However, often within a very short period of time, despite the best laid plans of staff, the patient and family become engaged in the same types of nongratifying interaction as before, even to the extent of again living together. This would seem to indicate that successful separation is a process over time that will need to involve all the relevant people.

When the difficulty clearly seems to be mainly intrapsychic, with relatively less impact on a marital or family system, as, for example, when someone lives by himself and not in close contact with his original family, individual therapy would probably be indicated. This is probably also the preferable modality for those who have difficulty in establishing intimate one-to-one relationships.

Of course, there will be many situations in which the situation is less clear cut, for example, for problems occurring in a first marriage. Then the therapist must use his judgment.

Group therapy is probably indicated in those situations in which a major part of the difficulty lies in problematic or unsatisfactory peer group relationships. For problems that exist between family units and larger community systems, help from social agencies other than family therapists might be most appropriate (see Table 1).

RELATIVE CONTRAINDICATIONS

The following should be considered as "relative" contraindications, inasmuch as the current state of the field precludes listing them as absolute contraindications to family therapy. There are no outcome studies to document which types of situations are least responsive to family intervention. Relative contraindications include the following (we have modified contraindications 1–6 from Ackerman[11]).

1. *Families in the process of breaking up.* If the family is irrevocably committed to dissolution—for example, if the actual process of divorce is going on—then it is unlikely that family therapy will be useful. This is because one of the prerequisites for successful family therapy is that the family want to stay together and the members be emotionally committed to each other. If the family members do not care about one another, they will fail in the therapy. This must be

differentiated from a type of marital counseling, for example, in which the counseling can go on in spite of an impending breakup, to help make a separation or divorce "less painful" to all family members.[12]

Inexperienced therapists, however, often seem to be overly pessimistic (as well as sometimes overly optimistic) about the changes that can be brought about in families. It is useful to keep in mind that marital couples or families may begin by talking about breaking up, and may appear much more chaotic in the early sessions than they will appear later. Many families start treatment by emphasizing their worst aspects, and one often has the immediate reaction during a first interview of throwing up one's hands, feeling that one is dealing with a hopeless situation.

However, more experience in general, together with more experience with any particular family, usually brings to light many more of the positive workable assets of the family that they themselves have been underplaying initially and that the therapist may have been overlooking at the beginning. The fact that the family comes for treatment should itself be taken as an indication potentially that they are seeking help for their difficulties.

If the marital partners were determined to break up or divorce, and if this were not a conflicted or difficult issue for them, with many ambivalences, they would see a divorce lawyer, rather than seek family therapy. It will often prove useful to clarify the fact that everyone in the family may be hurting, and has been struggling, relatively unsuccessfully, to find ways to ease their pain and disappointment.

Many family therapists claim that they do not take sides on the issue of whether or not a marital couple should separate. They feel that their role is rather to help the couple clarify their own feelings about this question, and also to give the couple an opportunity to think about separation or divorce as possible solutions, among others. (Often, marital partners have this as a hidden agenda, and may delay facing it until the therapist opens up the topic for discussion.)

Other therapists, however, feel that, by and large, divorce is not a solution to marital problems, in that the spouses often remarry partners very much like the previous one, and continue the same patterns. A few marital partners divorce and remarry each other again several times over. Everyone is familiar with marriages in which the spouses cannot seem to live stably together, but also cannot seem to stay separated. In such instances, therapists should take a stand against useless divorce and, instead, actively encourage trying to work out the current marriage.

2. *Unavailability of family members.* If one member is 200 miles away in college, this makes family therapy of the whole family unlikely. However, it must be stressed that the more forceful the therapist in insisting that all family members come, the more successful he will be in getting the entire family together. Family resistance to change is more crucial to cooperation than such factors as distance, finances, job hours, and so forth. The family therapist should adopt the attitude that all family members are expected to want to attend sessions. He should give attention to the benefits and rewards for each individual family member, as well as for the family system as a whole, from attendance at the family sessions. The absence or other resistance of family members to the sessions will be scrutinized by the experienced therapist for what it reveals about the important processes in the family.

    The question is often asked whether family therapy can be of help when one parent is absent through death, separation, divorce, or other reasons. Obviously, *marital* therapy cannot be done under such circumstances, but experience has suggested that much useful *family* help may be offered even in one-parent families.

3. *Families in which the psychopathology in one family member is such that it would prevent the family therapy from doing the work of therapy.* For example, an adult family member may have a history of chronic sociopathic behavior, such as, stealing or lying. Some therapists might not consider this a contraindication, but at the very least, dishonesty would constitute a serious handicap. If this occurs in a child, and appears to be more a symptomatic response to a family situation than an integral part of a chronic character pattern, family therapy would certainly be indicated.

    If one family member is extremely paranoid or manic or agitated, the approach of choice might be medication first, prior to the onset of family therapy. Once the identified patient has come under symptomatic control, then the family therapy can proceed.[13] Another possibility is to work with all family members except the one whose pathology prevents therapy from succeeding; this is clearly a second choice. Others (a minority) have argued that the acute symptoms are reflections of a crisis that is best handled by doing therapy during the course of the crisis, that is, by not waiting for symptom resolution.

4. *Families in which there is lying in the family as a whole.* There are some families whose whole way of life is oriented around conscious lying. Such a family makes family therapy extremely difficult, but not impossible.

5. *Families in which the symptoms to be changed are the result of organic disease in one member of the family.* For example, one

member has a tumor of the brain and is forgetful. Major attention would have to be directed toward treatment of the underlying organic disease. While no amount of family therapy will change the course of the tumor, it might help the family live more comfortably with their anguish. What might be changed are the reactions of the patient and the family to the symptoms.

6. *Families in which the presenting problem show no current emotional or behavioral consequences for the family.* There is apparently a small number of families who from time to time seem intent on dredging up the past at a time when there are no current crises going on. They do this to affix blame for past family failures or disappointments. In this situation, therapists have found that not much useful work can be done.

7. *Families in which the risks (or consequences) of treatment are worse than the benefits.* This requires a judgment that such a result, for example, divorce, would not be a desired outcome or would be worse than the symptoms that existed at the start of treatment, for example, headaches. These can be difficult decisions, and the therapist may involve the family members in considering possible consequences, and whether they wish to continue or abandon treatment.

Another example is the "Doll's House" marriage, a type of marriage defined as one in which there is an extremely unequal relationship, where one spouse's incompetence is required or encouraged by the other. It is extremely fragile and crisis-prone and often breaks down at a change of family situation, for example, birth of a child. Although family treatment is problematic and the results uncertain, the clinical impression is that therapy has a greater chance of success if the therapist basically respects the unequal framework and works to reestablish the equilibrium existing prior to the crisis.[14]

8. *Families in which the identified patient has a fixed physical dependence on alcohol, barbiturates, heroin, or other such drugs.* Family therapy does not seem to be successful as the primary mode of treatment in preventing physical dependence on drugs. It may be of help in the early stages before the pattern becomes well fixed, and even later in aiding the family members in understanding the condition and avoiding nonuseful interventions and responses.

In the abuse of drugs such as marijuana, LSD, and mescaline, in which physical dependence is not found, family therapy may have a more important role to play. It has been reasoned by some that family therapy may be necessary to induce the user to discontinue drugs, since the use of drugs is a result of family psychopathology.

This may be especially true for the adolescent drug user.

9. *Existence of an important, valid family secret that could not be brought out in the open,* but that precludes the possibility of the family's doing any constructive therapeutic work, for example, overt homosexuality of one of the spouses, or bigamy (see section in Chapter 9, on Family Secrets). On the other hand, revealing secrets may lead to major changes in the family organization.

10. *Unyielding, inflexible cultural, religious, or economic prejudices against any sort of outside intervention in the family system* would certainly also make family therapy difficult, if not impossible. In such cases, other alternatives can be offered, such as working with a clergyman or a community worker, with the family therapist as a consultant.

11. *Necessity of other modalities of psychiatric treatment* should also be considered. In some cases, one would want to wait until the identified patient has established a relationship with the therapist; this is especially true of adolescents. A psychotic patient who is paranoid might not be able to tolerate family therapy until he reconstitutes using phenothiazines; he would be too suspicious of the therapist to benefit.

12. *The availability and the type of therapist* are also important. Many therapists find themselves uncomfortable doing family therapy and, in our opinion, they should not force themselves to undertake it. If the therapist encounters significant "countertransference" problems in working with a particular family, this, too, would be a contraindication. Families to which the therapist has emotional ties, for example, as a relative, ex-boyfriend or girlfriend, or old friend, would also be a contraindication.

   The age, sex, and race of the therapist in relation to the type or needs of the family are, by themselves, in our experience usually not a significant impediment to therapy.

   Others[11] have suggested that the therapist must be able to be active, directive, and set limits in order to do family therapy. The notion is that letting the identified patient or other family members control the therapy will doom the therapy to failure. (We have more to say on this in the chapters on therapy.) Although this notion seems correct clinically, it too has not been tested.

In each of the above situations, critical judgment by the therapist of the capability of the individual, in the family to benefit, in spite of one or more contraindications, would be the factor most important in deciding whether or not to prescribe family therapy.

CONCLUSION

It should be clear that family therapy is an approach, rather than a single technique. It is a group of therapeutic interventions, all focusing on the family but directed toward a variety of specific therapeutic goals. Therefore, the relative importance of the particular indication or contraindication depends in large part on how much the therapist uses the family model for diagnosis and on the intended goals of the therapy.

At present, indications and contraindications for family therapy are based on ingenious hunches as to treatment efficacy in a specific situation and on clinical experience (a term defined by some as "making the same mistake for 30 years").

It seems that family therapy as now practiced has about the same success rate as does individual psychotherapy (see Chapter 12). This conclusion, however, is based upon limited evidence and does not help the therapist to choose one treatment over another. We would caution that final decision as to indications or contraindications should be withheld until controlled data comparing family therapy with other types of therapies are available.

REFERENCES

1. Group for the Advancement of Psychiatry. The Field of Family Therapy. Report No. 78. New York, Group for the Advancement of Psychiatry, 1970.
2. Bard M, Berkowitz B: A community psychology consultation program in police family crisis intervention: Preliminary impressions. International Journal of Social Psychiatry 15:209–215, 1969.
3. Jackson D D: Family practice: A comprehensive medical approach. Comprehensive Psychiatry 7:338–344, 1966.
4. MacNamara M: Family stress before and after renal homotransplantation. Social Work 14:89–98, 1969.
5. Kellner R: Family Ill Health. An investigation in General Practice. Springfield, Ill, Charles C Thomas, 1963.
6. Ard B N, Ard C C, (eds): Handbook of Marriage Counseling. Palo Alto, California, Science and Behavior Books, 1969.
7. Klemer R H: Counseling in Marital and Sexual Problems. Baltimore, Williams and Wilkins, 1965.
8. Vincent C D (ed): Readings in Marriage Counseling. New York, Thomas Y Crowell, 1957.
9. Masters W, Johnson V: Human Sexual Inadequacy. Boston, Little, Brown, 1970.
10. Greenberg I M, Glick I D, Match S, Riback S S: Family therapy: Indications and rationale. Arch Gen Psychiatry 10:7–25, 1964.

11. Ackerman N W: Family therapy, in Arieti S (ed): American Handbook of Psychiatry, vol III. New York, Basic Books, 1966, pp 201–212.
12. Toomim M: Structured separation with counseling: A therapeutic approach for couple in conflict. Family Process 11:299–310, 1972.
13. Guttman H: A contraindication for family therapy: The prepsychotic or postpsychotic young adult and his parents. Arch Gen Psychiatry 29:352–355, 1973.
14. Pittman F Flomenhaft K: Treating the Doll's House marriage. Family Process 9:143–155, 1970.

11

Family Treatment When the Identified Patient Has a Specific Psychiatric Diagnosis

OBJECTIVES

- To be aware of some of the family interaction patterns associated with families which have members with specific types of disturbances
- To be able to differentially treat such families

When the identified patient has a specified major psychiatric diagnosis, for example, schizophrenia, treatment of the individual may be relatively conventional (for example, phenothiazines for schizophrenia) with the addition of family therapy. It should be made clear that we will not be discussing here in any great detail each one of the diagnostic entities. (This information is available in standard textbooks of psychiatry.) Rather, we will indicate those specific problem areas that are of particular interest to a family therapist.

As indicated in the chapter on family evaluation, the family therapist attempts to deal with those issues relevant to the family's basic needs, the present stage of its life cycle, and its ability to carry out its important functions. At times the treatment will be largely dependent on the psychiatric diagnosis of the identified patient (such as manic-depressive psychosis) or on the individual character-types of the family members (such as alcoholism).

In many instances it will be necessary to treat both the specific condition(s) in the individual family member(s) and the problems in living together that are concomitant with, and perhaps related to, these conditions. Some of these family problems may be related to the causation of individual illness, some may be secondary to it, and others may not be so clearly connected. For example, if schizophrenia has developed in a spouse early in the marriage, the therapist's attention must be directed to treatment of the mental illness and to the nature of the marital interaction, past, present, and future, including its possible role in the illness. If there is a major psychiatric disorder in one of the family members, attention must be paid to the manifestations of the disorder which may be symptomatic of, or interfering with, the attempts to deal with the family's problems in living.

SCHIZOPHRENIA

This syndrome has been the most extensively studied by family therapists. An early, uncontrolled study of schizophrenic families by a group at Yale found the following characteristics in the 16 intensively studied schizophrenic families: failure to form a nuclear family; family schism and skew; blurring of generation lines; pervasion of the entire atmosphere with irrational, usually paranoid ideation; persistence of unconscious incestuous preoccupation; and sociocultural isolation.[1]

They described two types of family conflict patterns. In the "schismatic" family, the parents fill complementary roles, undercut each other and compete for the children. The family is in "two camps," and the identified patient cannot use one parent as a model for identification or as a love object without losing the support of the other parent. In the "skewed" family the psychopathology is dominant in one parent, that is, one parent is strong and the other is weak. The psychopathology is accepted or shared by the mate without any attempt to change it.

Wynne[2] has described what he calls "pseudomutuality" in schizophrenics' families. This is a type of relatedness in which there is a preoccupation of family members with fitting into former roles at the expense of individual identity. Such families lose their ability to test reality; that is, rather than see the world as it is, they strive for an agreed-upon interpretation. No divergence is allowed. Others have pointed out that some of the symptoms of schizophrenia can be understood as an attempt by the patient to become an individual, rather than to fit into the stereotyped, rigid mold of the family.[3]

Bateson and his coworkers have discussed a kind of communication pattern called the "double bind."[4,5] Five conditions are necessary for the double bind:

1. There must be two people who are significantly emotionally involved with one another.
2. It must be repetitive.
3. There must be a primary injunction.
4. There must be a secondary injunction, which contradicts the primary injunction.
5. There must be a tertiary injunction, which does not permit escape.

The classic example is the mother who walks over to her son (two people) and says to him (over and over again), "kiss me" (primary injunction) and then if he attempts to do this, moves away from him (secondary injunction) and then berates him for not being a good son (tertiary injunction). In other words, the identified patient is asked to respond to a communication that has an overt and covert message requiring mutually exclusive or incongruent responses. In a recent study of the double bind situation comparing parents of schizophrenics to parents of normal children, delinquents, and children with ulcerative colitis, the parents of schizophrenics gave the most invalid interpretation and disaffirmed their own or their spouses' interpretations most frequently.[6]

Most studies show a high incidence of serious pathology in the parents when there is schizophrenia in a child.[7] Lidz[8] has shown that one or both parents of schizophrenic patients have had or now have serious emotional problems. Wynne and Singer[9,10] have been able to identify disturbed styles of parental thinking, using their Rorschach test protocol with schizophrenic children compared to controls, using raters blind to diagnosis, although a recent study could not replicate this finding.[11]

A few studies suggest that the siblings of schizophrenics avoid becoming symptomatic either by constricting their personalities and family interactions or by openly rebelling and physically leaving the family.[12] Other observers have noted that the sibling is more independent, less troubled with decisions, and less involved with parents.

Other workers have noted that schizophrenic families have greater difficulty than normal ones in acknowledging conflict, and are much less flexible in problem solving;[13,14] that their interpersonal difficulties clearly interfere with problem solving;[15,16] that they are less adequate in communicating instructions and are more ambiguous;[17] and, finally, that they have more difficulty planning.[18] Moreover, problem solving is further handicapped because such families appear to utilize idiosyncratic views from within the family to the exclusion of those from without. Feelings are acted upon as though they were facts. Parents distort reality in the service of their own emotional needs, and infantilize their children to make themselves feel more mature. Laing and others[3] feel that the signs and symptoms of schizophrenia may be a "logical" adaptive response to an illogical family. Laing has used the term "mystification" to describe the family's negation and denial of the patient's experience.

However, as Mosher and Feinsilver have said,

> Major disagreement exists as to the relative *significance* of these findings. Such questions arise as, do the deviant interactional patterns observed antedate the occurrence of illness in one family member? And, if so, are they *causally* implicated in schizophrenia's development? Or do these deviant patterns simply stem from the parents' efforts to relate to their already strange offspring? (p. 21).[19]

We feel these studies have been provocative in opening the door to the study of the role of the family in the etiology of schizophrenia. Appropriate scientific controls are certainly needed to establish cause and effect relationships. The entire issue of interactional process and schizophrenia is discussed in detail in an extensive monograph by Mishler and Waxler.[20]

In the treatment of schizophrenic families, most therapists agree that except for the one-third of the schizophrenic patients who might remit spontaneously, there is no substitute for somatic therapy (that is, antipsychotic medication). However, the effect of the medication seems clearly to be related to the type of family the patient returns to; phenothiazines have been shown to decrease aggression in patients who come from families that have been characterized as "low tension and low conflict families." But there was no change in the patients who came from high conflict and tension homes.[21]

To the extent that the schizophrenia exists in the context of the family, one must look at what seems to be happening in the family. For example, often the late adolescent schizophrenic is "stuck" in attempting to separate from the family. One of the tasks of the family therapist is to assess the patient's strength, to see to what extent he seems able to separate from the family. The treatment goals may then revolve around these issues, to enable the separation to take place eventually, or to enable the patient to function better within the family.

Another task in treatment is the well documented communication difficulty in schizophrenic families.[22] Family members other than the identified patient, although they are not schizophrenic, seem to exhibit many peculiarities of communication, especially noticeable when the family group (even without the schizophrenic member present) attempts to communicate. The family as a whole seems often to have a more subtle thought disorder.[9,10] There often is difficulty in focusing attention and in goal-directedness. There is a pervasive sense of meaninglessness, and extensive use of "mind reading." (The therapist frequently hears of what others "really mean.") also there is much silence and lack of meaningful talk.

The therapist must, therefore, take some of the focus off the identified patient and put it onto the family and its dysfunctional patterns. The therapist has to be active and organized (to counter family disorganization), be able to encourage verbal (rather than nonverbal) communication, make clear who is communicating to whom, indicate goals and test reality. The therapist, in a sense, lends his own ego to the family, teaching the family how to communicate effectively. He helps the family members disagree with what is bizarre, or helps them to ask about something that they do not understand.

As simple as these techniques may seem to the beginner, it will be necessary to repeat them over and over in these families. It will be as important to straighten out the disturbed communication *process* as it will be to straighten out the *content*.

With the nationwide trend of treating schizophrenic patients in the community (rather than in state hospitals remote from the family), a large number of patients now live with their families or "significant others." There is thus now not only the patient's problem, but also the family's problem in living with one member who has a chronic illness that may markedly interfere with his ability to interact with others, to work, and so forth.[23-25] The nature of schizophrenia (as best as is known) and secondary reaction of family members to the identified patient may need to be explored, as may the importance of rehabilitative processes. The therapist must be sensitive to the family's denial of the identified patient's illness or (equally unfortunate) the family's treating the patient as if he were completely incompetent. A family hostile to the identified patient with schizophrenia can cause a relapse.[26]

There are two subtypes of schizophrenia that cause particular problems to family therapists and these are discussed below.

Paranoid Patients

An extremely difficult problem exists when one member of the family is paranoid, with such symptoms as suspiciousness, jealousy, evasiveness, excessive religiosity, irritability, and grandiosity. Appropriate medication is a problem because the patient often does not want to take it, fearing he will be "one down" in the family. If the patient will not take medications, some therapists will not see the patient. In the presence of paranoid patients, the therapist must be scrupulously open, not take sides, not deal behind the patient's back, and be sure all confidences are shared.

The paranoid patient may be frightened, belligerent, or frankly assaultive, either in the present or in the past. This factor must be taken into account, as usually little or no beneficial therapeutic work can take place in an atmosphere in which people are frightened for their physical safety.

Catatonic Patients

The catatonic patient also presents specific problems in that most commonly motor function is completely stopped. Often the family seems to acquiesce in the patient's nonfunctioning. We have seen some families in which they had tolerated the patient's sitting in his room not doing anything for 3 or 4 years. The therapist and family in these cases must be active and persistent in helping the patient to function. (It should be remembered that the mute catatonic is not deaf, dumb, or blind.) This often is a frustrating and difficult process. Behavior modification techniques involving the whole family have been tried.

MANIC-DEPRESSIVE ILLNESS

In these disorders, as in schizophrenia, there appears to be some genetic contribution. Nevertheless, both somatic and psychosocial treatment are often indicated. In acute stages of mania, for example, it is often mandatory to treat the patient with lithium and to see the family together in order to manage the patient's behavioral symptomatology, which is often quite inappropriate (for example, spending the life savings of the family). An analogous situation exists with the seriously depressed person who may be actively planning suicide. It is noteworthy that families will perceive changes in the identified patient following lithium treatment. Specifically, they perceive such a person to have fewer undesirable attributes than prior to treatment. They do not perceive more desirable attributes as being present.[27]

A crucial intervention is to help the family to recognize the earliest symptoms of recurrence of either depression or mania, and to seek help. The family is helped to see that the identified patient is not "bad" but has an "illness."

Some work has been done on the family patterns of manic-depressive disease. Both the identified patient and spouse feel weak and dependent, and both have a wish for the other to be strong.[28] The identified patient often marries a spouse who will control him or her. There is also a clinical belief that in families with a manic-depressive member there is a transmitted family difficulty or distortion in dealing with depressive affect. In some way, the patient represents this disability in extreme form, and because of extreme inability to cope with sadness may reverse the affect into mania. This notion is in some ways analogous to the theories of the transmission of irrational modes of thinking in the families of schizophrenic patients.

NEUROSIS

Some investigators emphasize the view that neurotic patterns arise in one's family of origin before formation of one's family of procreation. Others stress, conversely, that neurotic illness is a kind of contagious disease that can be transmitted from one marital partner to another,[29] or that the appearance of symptoms in one partner can most fruitfully be understood by looking at the marital system. In cases of obsessive-compulsive neurosis it is thought, from the family point of view, that the symptoms are ways of dealing with problems that cannot be expressed directly to another family member. In cases of school phobia, evidence seems to point to a difficulty of both mother and child separating from each other.[30] In conversion neurosis, the feeling has been that the somatic symptom is a displacement of a conflict between marital partners.

As to therapy, McDanald[31] believes that the best work can be done during "crisis times," when the family is motivated to change. He uses both individual and family therapy in treatment of neurosis. Other authors try treating the identified patient with individual psychotherapy and use family psychotherapy when individual therapy alone is not effective.

School phobias are ideal situations for family therapy. Most commonly, when mother and child do not want to separate there is often a problem existing between wife and husband that gets displaced onto the child. With all types of phobias, treatment of the individual by behavior modification should be considered. If that does not work, consideration should be given to family treatment, and possibly family behavior therapy.

PERSONALITY DISORDER

A common situation is one in which a marital couple enters therapy seemingly complaining of one or both member's basic character structure. Only later does the problem come to be seen as arising out of a change of family phase or an acute crisis in the family, such as loss of job. The changing of personality structure is extremely difficult by any method, but helping the family system to master its life cycle tasks or to live within the strengths and limitations of the two marital partners may be possible.

Patients with hysterical personality (histrionic personality disorder) are often excitable, unstable, overly reactive, self-dramatizing seductive, and attention-seeking. Such patients may marry obsessive-compulsive spouses, seeing in them strength, reliability and firmess (whereas, at times, all they may get is rigidity and coldness). There are usually marked sexual problems. Treatment of this disorder has been notably difficult with individual psychotherapy. Family therapy offers an alternative possibility[32] (of as yet uncertain value). From this vantage point, the obsessive-compulsive marital partner was attracted by what he took to be the partner's sociability and spontaneity, later finding that this seems more like disorganization and childishness. The obsessive-compulsive husband withdraws more and more, at the same time that the hysterical wife becomes more flamboyant in her behavior. Often, use of other mechanisms such as drug and/or alcohol abuse is common, and a vicious cycle is established. The goal of therapy may be to try to bring the couple back to where they were before this cycle was established. Sometimes, simple maneuvers may be helpful in educating the partners as to what will and will not work in dealing with this spouse, such maneuvers, for example, as suggesting that a husband bring a bouquet of roses to his wife, or pointing out to the wife that she should talk to her husband, rather than act.

Alcoholism

This disorder appears to have strong familial and cultural determinants. The family therapy literature suggests that it may be a way of dealing with conflicts (via withdrawal) that cannot be expressed directly with family members and that it allows the alcoholic to express feelings (for example, anger) that he cannot express to family members when he is not drinking.

It has also been thought that when the family member is drinking, he assumes a position of "one-upmanship" or control over the nonaffected family members. It is thus a way of sending a relationship-defining message while at the same time denying the message.[33]

In our experience, family therapy has been ineffective in changing the long-term course of the chronic, fixed alcoholic. This is not to suggest, however, that family therapy cannot be used to help the family adjust to it and improve family functioning where one family member is diagnosed as alcoholic.

Special notice should be taken of the observation that not all patients with alcoholism have a chronic course. Often, an intermittent increase in drinking is a response to a problem within the family. In these cases, it can be appropriately treated with family therapy. Care must be taken that the nonaffected spouse does not propagate the alcoholic patient's drinking.[34,35] The spouse is the supplier and the victim simultaneously. For example, in the D. family, where the wife was the identified patient having an alcohol problem, they came to treatment complaining they never went out together. After months of therapy, the husband took his wife to a wine-tasting festival. The script involves a continual reinactment of provocation, misbehavior, remorse, and atonement.

Drug Abuse

This problem has been the subject of much research over the past 10 years. There is a difference between chronic use of drugs causing physical dependence, such as barbiturates and heroin, and casual use of nonaddicting agents, such as marijuana and LSD. In our opinion, the former category is often extremely resistive to family therapy intervention. Such drug users are sometimes removed from their sociocultural milieu, and family therapy is not possible given this limitation. However, it should be pointed out that some facilities that are treating the nonaddicted drug user (even those with, for example, occasional mixed use of alcohol, marijuana, amphetamines, and psychedelics) use family therapy as a primary form of treatment based on the rationale that the drug use is a symptom of disturbed functioning and communication in the family.[36,37] One agency has reported better outcome for male heroin abusers using Multiple Family Group Therapy.[38]

Delinquency and Criminality

There has been a great deal written about this topic in the family literature. The problem of delinquency appears to be an extremely complex one involving social and cultural factors that have to be taken into account in any overall evaluation.

In studies of juvenile delinquency, some writers have pointed to the high incidence of absent or inadequate same-sexed parental role models. Some have described parental limit-setting that is either too lenient, too harsh, or extremely inconsistent. Others have posited a "negative identity" and "bad-me" self-image in many of these individuals.

It is thought that, in part, the delinquent behavior is preconditioned by parental covert expectations or overt approval. The child may get implicit cues to act in antisocial ways, together with explicit prohibitions against such activity. The unspoken message is, "Do it, but don't get caught!" There are thought to be "holes" in the parental conscience, which then lead to the identified patient's acting out the unconscious needs of the parents[39] which they cannot tolerate in their own behavior.

Criminal behavior in adults may be later residues of such earlier factors, and in either juvenile delinquency or adult criminality careful evaluation must be made to ascertain the extent to which patterns are acute or chronic, associated with stress or not, acceptable to the individual or not, and also, with respect to the possible use of family therapy, the involvement and interest of the family members in the antisocial individual. Such evaluation should differentiate those instances in which family therapy would be helpful from those in which it might be fruitless.

In the area of juvenile delinquency, family therapists have attempted to direct their intervention toward ameliorating the defects mentioned above. Analogous attempts would be instituted in the case of adult criminality.

Minuchin[40] views delinquency as a symptom of family disturbance. In working with delinquent families of low income, he sees the family in a room with a one-way mirror. He has one family member come outside to "observe the action." He focuses on getting the family to delay gratification by helping the family to discuss before acting on decisions. The therapist attempts to clarify the role structure of the family, which is often lacking. Environmental manipulation is a major technique. The therapist must be extremely active in the therapy, especially in helping to reduce blaming. Surprisingly, the identified patient often resists the work of family therapy and the therapist must counter the identified patient's self-destructive maneuvers.[41]

Maladaptive Sexual Behavior

Incest.   In many cases of frank incest, study of the family interactions involved seems to reveal a covert, and at times even an overt, acceptance by the wife of the sexual relationship between her husband and daughter. The mechanisms involved often are relatively complex, but at times they seem to get mother "off the hook," so far as sex is concerned.[42,43] The incestuous behavior can also serve to maintain the homeostasis of the family unit.

> The I. family sought help following discovery of an incestuous relationship between the father and the 14-year-old daughter. The mother sought help to find out "whether Max is a sex maniac and ought to be put away or whether he's just plain rotten and ought to be put in jail and divorced." Examination of the situation revealed that the mother and father had not been getting along for many years. Over the past 2 years, she had taken to leaving home after supper, telling her husband and daughter that she might be working all night, and she told them not to "get in trouble." The husband and daughter had then begun mutual petting prior to bedtime, which had progressed to intercourse.

Homosexuality. Many parents indicate a great deal of concern with respect to the possibility of one of their children growing up to be homosexual. Such concerns are often unrealistic, and even if based on good evidence, dispute exists as to what course to pursue with an adamantly homosexual individual. Books have been written to help parents in a prophylactic sense.[44] Much recent work dealing with the life history of homosexual patients has stressed factors in the family system as etiologic in the individual's homosexual development.[45]

Similarly, transvestism, transsexualism, and other sexual variants have been ascribed to particular patterns in the family of origin, and therefore, presumably amenable to one or another type of preventive family intervention.

Family treatment may be important in helping to deal with these often extremely difficult issues once they have surfaced into the family's awareness. Some families may be aided in accepting life-styles that cannot be changed, without disrupting positive and important relationships.

Illegitimate pregnancy. Many factors appear to be operative in this area as well. Family issues, such as adolescent rebellion against parental dictates, low self-esteem, and so forth, may at times be important, and when such issues are present, family therapy may be helpful in a preventive sense, as well as in increasing mutual acceptance and understanding.

Other sexual disorders. Disturbances of potency, orgastic competence, and other functional disorders of sexual intercourse are alluded to in Chapter 4, where the work of Masters and Johnson, and others, is mentioned. The sexual symptom is dealt with as a communication problem between the spouses. For example, frigidity or impotence can mean "I hate you," or "I'm scared of you." Treatment often must be both educational and interactional. There may be much ignorance and guilt with respect to sexual information and practices and these factors may interact in complex ways with those related to the nonsexual areas of the relationship. Both may require the therapist's attention.

THE FAMILY AND SOMATIC ILLNESS

A great deal of study over the last 10 years has been concerned with the influence of the family on the development and course of somatic illness and, conversely, the effect of somatic illness on the family. Although this area has been the subject of careful study for some time, it is still controversial. Some question the relationship between personality factors and physical illness, but many are convinced that such connections exist, even though the exact mechanisms may be obscure and the efficacy of psychosocial treatment interventions, including the family therapy, may not be firmly established.

In general, family researchers have observed that the development of some somatic illness (for example, ulcerative colitis) can be correlated with certain problems in family functioning (for example, symbiosis between the mother and the identified patient[46]). It is hypothesized that a breakdown in family homeostasis causes development of somatic symptoms in the member of the family who is most vulnerable at that time. What the causal mechanisms are between the family, the individual, and the somatic illness is not well understood.

Holmes[47] has demonstrated in controlled studies that the time of onset of somatic illness is associated with the kinds of life changes that are directly related to family functioning, for example, death of a spouse, divorce or separation, jail term, death of a close family member, personal illness or injury, marriage. Holmes' work documents for the first time psychosocial influences, that is, the family, in the etiology of somatic illness. For example, in the N. family, in which the maternal grandmother was dominant, the maternal grandfather died, and the mother developed tuberculosis. She later married a passive man. The oldest son, the mother's favorite, left the family at age 20, and the mother had a relapse of tuberculosis. The mother decompensated psychologically and physically, and the father developed an ulcer. The son rejoined the family, and the mother got better; when he left again, the mother developed arthritis.

THE FAMILY AND PSYCHOPHYSIOLOGICAL DISORDERS ("PSYCHOSOMATIC" ILLNESSES)

Psychophysiological disorders are defined as physical disorders of unknown etiology in which psychological factors are believed to play an important etiological role. This belief is based on frequent relation of emotional problems in the patient or his family to exacerbations of illness, and to the fact that somatic dysfunction often can be regarded as an exaggeration of the normal autonomic reactions to stress. These disorders are characterized by actual physical dysfunctions ("signs"). They usually involved a single organ system, for example, the gastrointestinal, and usually it is one that is under autonomic nervous system innervation. Occasionally more than one system is involved. The physiological changes involved are those that normally accompany certain emotional states (for example, when excited, increased gastric juice with hydrochloric acid is secreted). But in these disorders, the changes are more intense and sustained. Instead of being physiological, that is, adaptive, they become pathological, or maladaptive. The individual may not be consciously aware of relations between his illness and his family and cultural milieu. While there may or may not be structural changes, there must be demonstrable alterations of physiological function. By definition, psychophysiological disorders exclude psychological reactions secondary to medical illness (for example, the fear associated with cancer), purely psychogenic disorders like "conversion hysteria," and other diverse psychological situations that arise in medical practice (for example, chronic invalidism, psychogenic pain).

It has been suggested that in families in which psychophysiological illnesses exist, the families are rigid; the illness occurs after family stress events; the illness stabilizes the family system; and the mothers "label" the illness and the fathers collude in the process.[48] Often, the illness seems to serve as a mechanism to avoid looking at problems that exist within the family. For example, in the W. family, whenever Mr. W. wanted to talk about the budget Mrs. W. experienced a recurrence of migraine. Whenever she wanted to talk about his long business hours, he developed as asthmatic attack.

Specific correlative studies suggest a relationship between ulcerative colitis and, in one study, symbiosis between mother and identified patient[46] and, in another study, pseudomutuality in the family.[49] Another study found a correlation between asthmatic children and their mothers,[50] such that if asthmatic children were divided into two groups, those with strongly allergic features and those with weakly allergic features, the mothers fell into two groups also. The asthmatic children with strongly allergic features had relatively nonneurotic mothers, whereas the asthmatic children with nonallergic features had highly neurotic mothers. Such studies, in combination with others, suggest that a combination of constitutional and personality (individual and family) factors may be necessary conditions for the development of the somatic illness. One case has been reported of migraine as a reaction to "suppressed feelings of resentment" between family members, in which family therapy was used as the treatment of choice.[51] Similarly, Meyer and Haggerty[52] in a study of patients with Beta-hemolytic streptococcus infections found that both acute and chronic family stress was an important factor associated with development of disease.

Management of the somatic illness by the family physician should include an initial evaluation of the family situation. It should focus also on the development of the disease in the family context, similar illness in the nuclear or extended family, ways in which the disease affects the family daily life, and ways in which the family deals with the disease. All too often, however, the focus is solely on the identified patient with the somatic illness.

The next step, after careful evaluation, is to consider modifications in those family interaction patterns that seem to produce and exacerbate the illness. At the same time, the family should be encouraged to get appropriate medical help. The presumed danger in this approach is that with psychological exploration of the individual or the family, the physical illness may be exacerbated. Of course, close collaboration with the primary physician is mandatory.

THE FAMILY AND OTHER MEDICAL PROBLEMS

Other medical problems *without* a presumed family etiological role, initially presenting and commonly seen in medical practice (for example, intractable asthma[53] or "brittle diabetes"), have been managed with a focus on the family. For example, disagreements between spouses correlate with the onset of the attack of asthma or diabetic coma in the identified patient.

The Effects of Somatic Illness on the Family

Primary physicians have long recognized that any illness in an individual family member, especially chronic and/or severe illness, will affect the family system. Changes in an individual's role function, ambulation, earning power, sex drive, and independence inevitably will evoke more or less adaptive coping mechanisms on the part of the rest of the family. For example, the illness of cardiac and "stroke" patients, patients with severe arthritis, patients who are on renal dialysis or who receive renal transplantation, creates symptoms not only in the patient but also in the family.[54] Likewise, the family that has one member dying of a disease with associated prolonged medical and surgical intervention often will have trouble coping with such an overwhelming family stress. Adjustment of all the above situations has been aided through the use of a family therapy approach.

Anorexia Nervosa

Several case reports have suggested that anorexia nervosa is a reaction of the identified patient to problems in the family. Family therapy is used in the service of changing patterns in the family that prevent the identified patient's regaining lost weight.[55-57]

HOW THE FAMILY USES A MEDICAL PROCEDURE
IN AN ATTEMPT TO CHANGE THE FAMILY

The family physician often must decide when to perform a procedure for which there is no medical necessity, but which the patient has requested. For example, a wife wants oral contraceptives or a husband wants a vasectomy in order to have extramarital relations without the risk of pregnancy. This behavior is often secondary to an intramarital problem. Although "there is no rule of law that states that one spouse can prevent the other from receiving medical care that is desired, there also does not appear to be any legal rule that states that one spouse must always be informed of medical care received by the other"[58] (p. 505). The point is, however, that family members often inappropriately use the physician in attempts to solve underlying family problems. Obvious management is to meet with the entire family and, once the family problem is understood, to intervene from a family point of view, rather than proceeding first with the medical procedure.

Family Interaction Patterns
and Medical Consultation

A number of recent studies have suggested that certain patterns of family interaction influence a family member's decision to seek medical help, using symptoms such as colds or urinary frequency as the ticket of admission. Kellner[59] studied all the families in his general practice who had at least one family member with overt emotional illness or a functional symptom. In one-third of such families, he believed that the illness of one family member (usually the mother) caused symptoms in another (usually a child). Both patients and their relatives in the "neurotic" families had higher attendance rates and a higher incidence of physical illness than patients and relatives from "nonneurotic" families.

Part of the author's conclusions are as follows: "The effect of illness in the family seems to depend on its severity, duration, and type, on the emotional bond between patient and the relative, and on the susceptibility of the latter" (p. 77). He also points out that "it seems that illness in the family, chiefly severe and prolonged illness, can make the relatives unhappy or afraid or can produce a preoccupation with disease. This may induce them to consult their general practitioner more often; it may sometimes precipitate neurotic symptoms or psychosomatic disorders, and perhaps predispose to physical illness" (p. 79). Illness of whatever kind and combination in one family member affects others and is in turn directly related to the physical-emotional well-being of other family members.

MENTAL RETARDATION

The term mental retardation comprises a variety of etiological possibilities, but in most instances there are inevitable secondary family problems.

In addition to the real problems of social development and functioning of the identified patient owing to his possibly damaged biological equipment, there are the associated, often maladaptive, family reactions. The family feels a sense of rejection, a sense of guilt, often social isolation, and actual anxiety about caring for the child's usual health needs.[60] Family members may make the child with mental retardation a scapegoat, to cover up unresolved conflicts between mother and father, or between parent and child.[61] Help must be focused on both the identified patient's specific needs and on his family's attitudes and behavior.

DISORDERS OF CHILDHOOD AND ADOLESCENCE

This includes such diverse entities as childhood schizophrenia, autism, neurotic traits, and adjustment reactions of childhood and adolescence. The field of child psychiatry recognizes the importance of the family, both theoretically and practically. It often does so on the basis of concepts first worked out for individual dynamics and therapy. It uses an individual psychotherapeutic model, with collateral therapy for the parents, in which family members are seen individually by one or more therapists. Often, only several key family members are seen, rather than all the members of the family jointly. However, in the last few years, there has been a change in that pattern,[62] and now some children's clinics are using the concepts and techniques of conjoint family therapy.

With respect to the distressed mid-to-late adolescent, a common view is that family therapy is relevant as part of an overall treatment program, to the extent that the adolescent is still living at home or is still financially, emotionally, or otherwise tied to his family of origin. On the other hand, for the adolescent who has become more autonomous in these respects, family therapy will be less indicated, and more emphasis will be placed on either individual or group psychotherapy.

CHILD ABUSE[63]

This term covers a variety of syndromes, from the actually "battered" child (including burns, multiple fractures, and death) to "failure to thrive." Epidemiologically the problem is not restricted to low socioeconomic classes, but occurs among all races and all socioeconomic classes. Pediatricians feel that the central problem is that mothering is not "turned on" for various reasons usually related to other familial or social problems. The baby's cry is perceived by the mother as a criticism. The mother becomes angry and tries to punish the baby in retaliation for what the parent interprets as a rejection. The immediate consequence to the infant is that he is physically and/or psychologically hurt at a time when he is helpless. If the infant can survive without serious injury or death, the presumed psychological sequel is that he becomes very fearful, unusually anxious to please adults, and develops school problems. When the child grows older there is inversion of the parent-child role—the child feels, "What can I do to make my parent happier so that he will stop hitting me"; the parent feels "What is wrong with this child?" Often, the parents themselves were rejected or battered as children. In about 10 percent of the cases, at least one parent is psychotic.

In approximately 80 percent of the cases, early identification of the problem can make it possible for the child to remain in the home. Overall mortality is about 40 to 50 percent in untreated cases; even with family intervention, there is a 10 percent mortality, but in most cases, with family intervention rebattering can be cut to almost zero. Where the battering parent is psychotic, removal from the home usually is indicated.

It must be stressed that repeated visits by the mother with the battered child to the emergency room pediatrician or internist is a cry for family intervention. In such early stages, seeking to provide the battering parent with insight into the family dynamics is contraindicated and leads to guilt in the parent and termination of the treatment contract.

REFERENCES

1. Fleck S: Family dynamics and origin of schizophrenia. Psychosomatic Medicine 22:333–344, 1960.
2. Wynne L C, Ryckoff I, Day J, Hirsch S I: Pseudo-mutuality in the family relations of schizophrenics, in Bell N W, Vogel E F (eds): A Modern Introduction to the Family. Glencoe, Illinois, Free Press, 1960, 573–594.

3. Laing R D, Esterson S: Families and schizophrenia. International Journal of Psychiatry, 4:65–71, 1967.
4. Bateson G, Jackson D D, Haley J, Weakland J: Towards a theory of schizophrenia. Behav Sci 1:251–264, 1956.
5. Bateson G, Jackson D D, Haley J, Weakland J H: A note on the double bind—1962. Family Process 2:154–161, 1963.
6. Sojit C: The double bind hypothesis and the parents of schizophrenics. Family Process 110:53–74, 1971.
7. Alanen Y: The families of schizophrenic patients. Proc Roy Soc Med 63: 227–231, 1970.
8. Lidz T, Fleck S, Alanen Y O, Cornelison A: Schizophrenic patients and their siblings. Psychiatry 26:1–18, 1963.
9. Wynne L C, Singer M T: Thought disorder and family relations of schizophrenics. I. A research strategy. II. A classification of forms of thinking. Arch Gen Psychiatry 9:191–206, 1963.
10. Singer M T, Wynne L C: Thought disorder and family relations of schizophrenics. III. Methodology using projective techniques. IV. Results and implications. Arch Gen Psychiatry 12:187–212, 1965.
11. Hersch S, Leff J: Parental abnormalities of verbal communication in transmission of schizophrenia. Psychol Med 1:118–127, 1971.
12. Lidz T, Fleck S, Cornelison A: Schizophrenia and the Family. New York, International Universities Press, 1965.
13. Lerner P: Resolution of intrafamilial role conflict in families of schizophrenic patients. I. Thought disturbance. J Nerv Ment Dis 141:342–351, 1966
14. Lerner, P: Resolution of intrafamilial role conflict in families of schizophrenics patients. II. Social maturity. J Nerv Ment Dis 4:336–341, 1967.
15. Reiss D: Individual thinking and family interaction. III. An experimental study of categorization performance in families of normals, those with character disorders, and schizophrenics. J Nerv Ment Dis 146:384–404, 1968.
16. Reiss D: Individual thinking and family interaction. IV. A study of information exchange in families of normals, those with character disorders, and schizophrenics. J Nerv Ment Dis 149:473–490, 1969.
17. Levin G: Communicator-communicant approach to family interaction research. Family Process 5:105–116, 1966.
18. Haley J: Research on family patterns: An instrument measurement. Family Process 3:41–65, 1964.
19. Mosher L, Feinsilver D: Special Report: Schizophrenia. U. S. P. H. S. Publication No. (HSM)72–9007. Washington, D. C., U. S. Government Printing Office, 1971.
20. Mishler E, Waxler N: Family Process and Schizophrenia. New York, Science House, 1968.
21. Cohen M, Freedman N, Engelhardt D, Margolis R A: Family interaction patterns, drug treatment, and change in social aggression. Arch Gen Psychiatry 19:50–56, 1968.
22. Feinsilver D: Communication in families with schizophrenic patients. Arch Gen Psychiatry 22:143–148, 1970.

23. Brown G, Birley J, Wing J: Influence of family life on the course of schizophrenic disorders: A replication. Br J Psychiatry 121:241–258, 1972.
24. Strauss J, Carpenter W: The prediction of outcome in schizophrenia. Arch Gen Psychiatry 27:739–746, 1972.
25. Vaillant G: The natural history of the remitting schizophrenias. Am J Psychiatry 120:367–375, 1963.
26. Hoenig J: Reaction of family studied in schizophrenics' home care. Psychiatric News August 15, 1973, p 22.
27. Demers R, Davis C: Influences of prophylactic lithium treatment on marital adjustment of manic-depressives and their spouses. Compr Psychiatry 12: 348–353, 1971.
28. Wadeson H, Fitzgerald R: Marital relationship in manic-depressive illness. J Nerv Ment Dis 153:180–196, 1971.
29. Buck C W, Ladd K L: Psychoneurosis in marital partners. Brit J Psychiatry 3:587–590, 1965.
30. Pittman F, Langsley D, DeYoung C: Work and school phobias: A family approach to treatment. Am J Psychiatry 124:1535–1541, 1968.
31. McDanald E C: Out-patient therapy of neurotic families, in Cohen I M (ed): Family Structure, Dynamics and Therapy. Psychiatric Research Report No. 20. Washington, D. C., American Psychiatric Association, 1966, pp 206–211.
32. Barnett J: Narcissism and dependency in the obsessional-hysteric marriage. Family Process 10:75–83, 1971.
33. Gorad S, McCourt W, Cobb J: The communications approach in alcoholism. Q J Stud Alcohol 32:651–668, 1971.
34. Deniker P, De Saugy D, Ropert M: The alcoholic and his wife. Compr Psychiatry 5:374–384, 1964.
35. Rae J: The influence of the wives on the treatment outcome of alcoholics: A followup study at two years. Br J Psychiatry 120:601–613, 1972.
36. Ganger R, Shugart G: The heroin addict's pseudoassertive behavior and family dynamics. Social Casework 57:643–649, 1966.
37. Rosenberg C: The young addict and his family. Br J Psychiatry 118:469–470, 1971.
38. Hendrix W: Use of multifamily counselling groups in treatment of male neurotic addicts. International Journal of Group Psychotherapy 21:84–90, 1971.
39. Szurek S: Some lessons from efforts at psychotherapy with parents. Am J Psychiatry 109:291–295, 1952.
40. Minuchin S, Auerswald E, King C, Rabinowitz C: The study and treatment of families that produce multiple acting-out boys. Am J Orthopsychiatry 34:125–134, 1964.
41. Minuchin S, Montalvo B: Techniques for working with disorganized low socioeconomic families. Am J Orthopsychiatry 37:880–887, 1967.
42. Lustig N, Dressen J, Spellman S, Murray T: Incest. Arch Gen Psychiatry 14:31–41, 1966.
43. Machotka P, Pittman F S, Flomenhaft K: Incest as a family affair. Family Process 6:98–116, 1967.

44. Wyden P: Growing Up Straight. New York, Stein and Day, 1968.
45. Brown D: Homosexuality and family dynamics. Bulletin of the Menninger Clinic 27:227–232, 1963.
46. Titchener J L, Riskin J, Emerson R: The family in psychosomatic process: A case report illustrating a method of psychosomatic research. Psychosom Med 22:127–142, 1960.
47. Holmes T S, Holmes T H: Short-term intrusion into the life style routine. J Psychosom Res 14:121–132, 1970.
48. Grolnick L: A family perspective of psychosomatic factors in illness: A review of the literature. Family Process 11:457–486, 1972.
49. Jackson D D, Yalom I: Family homeostasis and patient change, in Masserman J (ed): Current Psychiatric Therapies, vol IV. New York, Grune & Stratton, 1964, pp 155–165.
50. Block J: Parents of schizophrenic, neurotic, asthmatic, and cogenitally ill children. Arch Gen Psychiatry 20:659–674, 1969.
51. Vosburg R: Conjoint therapy of migraine: A case report. Psychosom 13:61–63, 1972.
52. Meyer R, Haggerty R: Streptococcal infection in families. Factors altering individual susceptibility. Pediat 29:539, 1962.
53. Liebman R, Minuchin S, Baker L: The use of structural family therapy in the treatment of intractable asthma. Am J Psychiatry 131:535–540, 1974.
54. Kossoris P: Family therapy: An adjunct to hemodialysis and transplantation. Am J Nurs 70:1730–1733, 1970.
55. Barca A: Family therapy and treatment of anorexia nervosa. Am J Psychiatry 128:286–290, 1971.
56. Bruch H: Family transaction and eating disorders. Compr Psychiatry 12:238–248, 1971.
57. Crisp A, Toms D: Primary anorexia nervosa, or a weight phobia in the male: Report of 13 cases. Br Med J 1:334–337, 1972.
58. Berger R P: Questions and answers. JAMA 228:505, 1974.
59. Kellner R: Family Ill Health: An Investigation in General Practice. Springfield, Ill, Charles C Thomas, 1963.
60. Adams M: Social aspects of the medical care for the mentally retarded. N Engl J Med 286:635–638, 1972.
61. Vogel E F, Bell N W: The emotionally disturbed child as the family scapegoat, in Bell N W, Vogel E F (eds): A Modern Introduction to the Family. Glencoe, Ill., Free Press, 1960, pp. 382–397.
62. Mendelbaum A: Family process in diagnosis and treatment of children and adolescents. Bulletin of the Menninger Clinic 35:153–166, 1971.
63. Kempe C, Helfer R: Helping the Battered Child and His Family. Philadelphia, Lippincott, 1972.

12

Family Treatment
and the Psychiatric Hospital

OBJECTIVES

- To understand the role of the family in the psychiatric hospitalization of one of its members
- To be able to treat such a family with the goal of preventing rehospitalization
- To become aware of family approaches and alternatives to hospitalization

The traditional view of the family that has one member in a psychiatric hospital was to view its members as, at best, purveyors of historical information to the social worker and payers of the bills, and, at worst, as malignant, pathogenic individuals who had played a major role in causing the patient's symptoms and who tended to make nuisances of themselves by interfering with the patient's treatment by the hospital staff.

The staff acted *in loco parentis,* and often inappropriately blamed the family for the patient's symptoms. The family was frequently not allowed to visit during the early part of the hospitalization. The psychiatric hospital was associated with much fear and stigma, and in many cases families were only too happy to stay away. In addition, prior to the availability of effective somatic treatments, hospital stays were much longer than currently, and already fragile family ties were broken.

In other cultures families are sometimes considered a vital part of the psychiatric hospitalization of any of their members. Because of a scarcity of trained professionals, families are needed in the hospital to care for the needs of the identified patient. They, in fact, often stay with the patient in or near the hospital. The assumption in such other cultures is that the patient is an integral part of the family network and it is relatively unthinkable that the patient would return anywhere else but to the family.[1]

ROLE OF THE PSYCHIATRIC HOSPITAL

The modern role of the hospital in relation to the families of psychiatric patients includes, first, temporarily removing the identified patient from a "pathogenic" environment (that is, one that constantly exacerbates the patient's symptoms) when it seems no longer possible to contain the situation by other means. In acute individual and family crises, and in emergency situations, hospitalization may be a means of decreasing behavioral eruptions. This may offer some substantial relief in a desperate family plight that is headed for serious deterioration. This enforced separation is undertaken with the goal of evaluating and changing the conditions so as to improve the family's patterns of interaction.[2] Second, hospitalization can be used to involve the family members in a controlled, structured setting that allows for continual observation and discussion of relevant family patterns. This permits establishment of motivation for seeking marital and family treatment after the patient has left the hospital, and preparation for the patient's return to a better functioning family setting. It may also set the stage for consideration of separation, where appropriate, in deadlocked marital or parent-child interactions.

Involvement of the family also makes possible the avoidance of staff overidentification with the patient against the family, the reduction of the stigma of psychiatric hospitalization, and the establishment of motivation for aftercare following hospitalization. It also allows family members to stay together where one member has to be hospitalized, as in postpartum psychosis, where mother and child have remained together on the ward.

FAMILY INFLUENCES ON HOSPITALIZATION

From a family point of view, the processes leading to hospitalization have been understood in a variety of ways.

1. The family is in a crisis and the hospitalization represents an attempt to solve the crisis.[3-5] In this connection, surprisingly, couples in retrospect have described the outcome of the psychotic episode and

their attempts to cope with it as a strongly positive experience for the family.[6]

2. The family extrudes the identified patient from the family, an attempt to solve the crisis.[7]

3. The family uses the hospital to get treatment for a member other than the identified patient. Experience has shown that the hospitalized member is not necessarily the only "sick" one (or at times, not even the "sickest" one) in the family. A family approach allows for the observation and evaluation of all significant others, with appropriate treatment (including medication) for the group and for nonpatient individuals who may require it. Therapists concentrating on the treatment of one individual may entirely overlook even gross, florid psychological disturbance in a close relative. When a therapist views his role as that of therapist to the family unit, this sort of blind spot is much less likely to occur.

4. The family uses the hospital as a resource to regain a "lost" member. For example, a father who drinks and is never home is finally convinced to go into a hospital because of his drinking. The family's motivation is to have him back as a functioning father and spouse (on the other hand, sometimes the family needs to keep him "sick" for its own needs).

5. The hospital is used as a neutral arena to change longstanding maladaptive patterns of family functioning.

If these assumptions about influences of hospitalization are valid, then it follows that in such cases the treatment program is inadequate unless it includes the family.

FAMILY TREATMENT BY THE HOSPITAL TEAM[8,9,10,11]

Work with the family must start very early, preferably prior to hospitalization, when the family is trying to arrange admission, or at the time of actual admission. Many hospital personnel have had the experience of beginning discharge planning late in the course of hospitalization only to discover at that time that the family resists having the patient home. It may be explicitly pointed out to the family that hospital treatment of the identified patient involves treatment of all family members. This may be made a condition of admission.

Family therapy can be combined with other methods of treatment, such as individual therapy, drug therapy, and so forth (see Chapter 7). Multiple family (or marital) group therapy has become an integral part of inpatient treatment programs. Receiving support, encouragement, and sharing of common problems with other families allows such families to get involved and gain understanding.

The hospital milieu is especially advantageous for observing and pointing out family interaction patterns. For example, if an adolescent child is paranoid about the nursing staff, it may be demonstrated to him that this is similar to the way he reacts to his mother. Accurate observation of the family may reveal that the patient has some good reasons for his symptoms.

Family therapy has been carried out by all members of the hospital treatment team. If in addition to the formal family treatment sessions the family participates in hospital activities, they are enabled to see their role in action. This is important in getting the family actually to modify their actions, rather than just talk about them. Nurses, at visiting time or other scheduled times, can meet with the patient and family to modify the family system. Occupational therapists have prescribed family treatment oriented around work behavior. For example, the family can prepare a meal together. Recreational therapists have prescribed family recreational therapy, for example going on a picnic together. All these workers have crucial roles in changing longstanding behavior patterns in the family system.

POSTHOSPITAL FAMILY TREATMENT

Since one of the goals of hospitalization is to improve function of the identified patient and the family after completion of hospital stay, family therapy sets the stage for such a change. It allows for unadaptive family patterns to be changed in the hospital and to be tried out prior to discharge.[12] It prevents family resistance to having the identified patient at home. Most importantly, it enables families to get into treatment who might ordinarily resist beginning treatment. Thus, when the identified patient leaves the hospital, family treatment continues. Clinical impressions indicate that such family treatment may decrease the risk of subsequent hospitalization.

OTHER TYPES OF FAMILY INVOLVEMENT AS AN
ALTERNATIVE TO PSYCHIATRIC HOSPITALIZATION

At times of family crisis, psychiatric hospitalization of a family member is one solution. With the gradual shift of psychiatric services out of the hospital into the community, other alternatives have emerged. Pasamanick et al.[13,14] as long ago as 1967 reported being able to keep schizophrenic patients out of hospitals altogether by keeping the patients at home and sending the treatment team to them. Zwerling and Mendelsohn [15] used day hospitalization with a focus on family treatment as an alternative to psychiatric hospital admission. Langsley and Kaplan[5] were able to use family crisis therapy to prevent hospitalization, using the rationale that a change in the balance of family forces had precipitated the request for hospitalization, and understanding the shift could result in strategies to prevent extrusion of the identified patient. Although hospitalization can be prevented, it should be stressed that continued family work is needed to change behavior patterns that prevent the identified patient from functioning.

REFERENCES

1. Bell J, Bell E: Family participation in hospital care for children. Children 17:154–157, 1970.
2. Robiner E, Malminski H, Gralnick A: Conjoint family therapy in the inpatient setting, in Gralnick A (ed): The Psychiatric Hospital as a Therapeutic Instrument. New York, Brunner/Mazel, 1969, pp 160–177.
3. Sampson H, Messinger S, Towne R D: Family processes and becoming a mental patient. Am J Sociol 68:88–96, 1962.
4. Sampson H, Messinger S, Towne R D: The mental hospital and family adaptations. Psychiatr Q 36:704–719, 1962.
5. Langsley D, Kaplan D: The Treatment of Families in Crisis. New York, Grune & Stratton, 1968.
6. Dupont R, Ryder R, Grunebaum H: Unexpected results of psychosis in marriage. Am J Psychiatry 128:735–739, 1971.
7. Bursten B: Family dynamics, the sick role, and medical hospital admissions. Family Process 4:206–216, 1965.
8. Burks H, Serrano A: The use of family therapy and brief hospitalization. Dis Nerv Syst 26:804–806, 1965.
9. Fleck S: Psychotherapy of families of hospitalized patients, in Masserman J (ed): Current Psychiatric Therapies, vol III. New York, Grune & Stratton, 1963, pp 211–218.
10. Laqueur H P, La Burt H A: Family organization on a modern state hospital ward. Ment Hyg 48:544–551, 1964.
11. Lennard H, Epstein L J: Effects of psychoactive drugs on family behavior. Am J Orthopsychiatry 38:236 (abstr.) 1968.
12. Tauber G: Prevention of posthospital relapse through treatment of relatives. Journal of Hillside Hospital 13:158–169, 1964.
13. Pasamanick B, Scarpitti F, Dinitz S: Schizophrenics in the Community. New York, Appleton-Century-Crofts, 1967.
14. Davis A, Dinitz S, Pasamanick B: The prevention of hospitalization in schizophrenia: Five years after an experimental program. Am J Orthopsychiatry 42:375–388, 1972.
15. Zwerling I, Mendelsohn M: Initial family reactions to day hospitalization. Family Process 4:50–63, 1965.

13

Results of Family Therapy

OBJECTIVES

- To appreciate the kinds of results that can be expected from family and marital therapy in general, by age group, and by type of diagnosis of identified patient
- To appreciate the current "state of the art" of evaluation of outcome in marital and family therapy

Family therapy is a relatively new approach; it has been on the scene for about 15 years. As with most new psychiatric treatments, workers tend to become overenthusiastic about their results.[1] Ten years ago, the first case reports on the outcome of family therapy appeared, and at the end would sometimes be appended small notes reporting "outstanding results." These reports were useful in helping to advance the cause, but were of relatively little value in evaluating the effects of therapy. At the very least, they seemed to suggest that the treatment was not making the problem worse.

Later, larger series were reported.[2,3,4] Most of these studies indicated that family therapy was a "good" form of treatment. However, even at present, we have only a few carefully controlled studies.[5,15] By "controlled" is meant a study that includes, for example, randomization procedures and comparison with control groups receiving no treatment and/or other forms of treatment.

OUTCOME OF FAMILY THERAPY AS JUDGED
BY THE THERAPIST

Jackson and Weakland[6] reported on their work with 18 schizophrenics and their families, 4 of the patients being acutely ill, and 14 chronically ill. Seven patients were hospitalized at the outset of family therapy; of these, at the time of the report one was still in the hospital, three were living at home and able to go out unaccompanied, two were at home and working, and one was living alone, caring for her child and working part time. Six or seven showed a noticeable improvement in social adaptation and independence. Of the remaining 11 patients, 9 were young people, most of whom were not hospitalized, were living with their parents, and were restricted to the home. If they were able to go out, they were not functional. All but two of these improved to a degree that enabled them to start school again, to change from failure to passing, to start working, or to start going out of their homes unaccompanied. The remaining two patients who had been confined to their homes after discharge from the hospital showed similar changes.

MacGregor[7] reported that his preliminary results suggested that a method of treatment was being developed having results comparable to those of established conventional methods. Forty-three of 50 cases treated described family self-rehabilitative processes as having been effectively mobilized. In seven, the presenting picture was unchanged or worse. In 1964 MacGregor[2] reevaluated families who had undergone Multiple Impact Therapy 6 and 18 months earlier, to determine the status of the problem areas they originally presented. A variety of data were gathered, including interview and case history material. When the cases were analyzed, 49 families were judged to have improved and 13 failed to improve. This proportion varied as a function of family type, improvement being greatest for the "intimidated" neurotic and schizophrenic children, and poorest for the "immature, aggressive, autocratic character disorders" and rebellious, acting-out delinquent children.

Carroll et al.[8] reported on results of marital therapy in cases in which prolonged individual therapy had wholly or partially failed, stating that "of the six cases seen, four made significant gains, while the other two were unimproved" (p. 28).

Greenberg and coworkers[9] reported the results of 20 patients seen in family treatment, of whom 14 were diagnosed as schizophrenic, 2 as sociopathic personalities, 2 as depressive neurotics, 1 with manic-depressive disease, and 1 with a chronic organic brain syndrome. Age range was bimodal, with two clusters centering at about 41 and 20 years. All were inpatients treated with milieu therapy, individual therapy, and drug therapy, in addition to family therapy. In general, there was a "definite trend toward a favorable outcome." A follow-up study 6 months later located 13 patients (4 women and 9 men). All were functioning at work or school or working adequately as housewives, in contrast to their prehospital performance (being unable to work or function). Ten out of 13 had improved recreational and social activities. Five of the identified patients were getting along well with their families, three fairly well, and three in a kind of "metastable (changing) equilibrium" were living with their families, but were not happy about it. In two cases, the outcome was uncertain, both patients were thinking of leaving their spouses. There was significant remission of presenting symptomatology in all 13 cases, with one possible exception.

Schreiber[10] reported on family therapy with personality disorders in which the identified patients were children. There were 72 families; of these, 13 dropped out, 30 improved, and 29 showed no improvement. This must be compared with other forms of therapy for personality disorders, in which improvement rates are about the same.

Fitzgerald[11] has reported on results of marital therapy in a private practice setting. Of 49 couples, followed for 2½ years, there was a 75 percent improvement rate on termination of therapy on a 6-month follow-up. This was about equal to results with individual psychotherapy. However, family therapy was superior in that the length of treatment was less, as was the cost. The marital relationship was more improved, and there was a decreasing chance of the spouse doing worse following termination of therapy. On the other hand, in terms of the mental health of the patient as an individual, the individual approach would seem to be superior, according to Fitzgerald.

OUTCOME OF FAMILY THERAPY AS MEASURED BY INDEPENDENT MEASUREMENT INSTRUMENTS

One of the first measurements of outcome was by Chance,[12] who tested 24 families before and after treatment in which the treatment was individual treatment for father, mother, and patient, *with no conjoint sessions.* She clearly showed that there were rearrangements, in that the parents showed less "passive hostility" and more "active mastery," but there was no change in the overall "power hierarchy" of the family.

Spiegel and Sperber[13] did a 6-month follow-up of seven families, each of whom had received six family therapy sessions, and results showed that of the identified patients (children) there was total improvement of the presenting problems in two and partial improvement in the remaining five. However, of five families who responded to a checklist form, all parents felt that their children had become worse, although the study indicated that they had improved.

Minuchin et al.[14] evaluated an experimental group of 12 families in which the identified patient was a delinquent child. Testing with assigned verbal tasks showed no changes after treatment in the ability of the family to conceptualize integrative family activity other than eating or informal communication variables. The investigators did feel that there was greater clarity in certain aggressive tasks (previously denied), greater ability to express feelings toward others in the family, and better parental leadership in response to children. Significantly, the children were better able to express the need for parental leadership and there were fewer family fights (the majority of these being among siblings).

Alexander and Parsons[15] have been able to demonstrate a significant decrease in recidivism at the end of therapy and at 6- and 18-month follow-up, in delinquent families treated with family therapy compared to three types of controls. The family therapy was designed to increase family reciprocity and clarity of communication and to change family patterns of behavior. Changes in family interaction were associated with decrease in rates of recidivism.

Haley[16] compared six families treated with family therapy to six control families, but found no significant outcome differences in "evenness of participation" (that is, how much time each family member talked). Ferreira and Winter[17] found no changes in families compared before and after 6 months of family treatment using a test-retest designed on the variables of spontaneous agreement, decision time, and representation in the final family decisions.

An unpublished dissertation by Ayers reported by Winter[18] revealed that in comparing ten parents of disturbed children who received 16 hours of weekly family therapy with parents on a waiting list, using the interpersonal system of personality diagnosis and the Family Concept Q-Sort, the treated parents found themselves "*more* hostile and *more* dissatisfied with their families, whereas the waiting list group expressed more satisfaction with their child after being kept waiting!" (p. 112). One interpretation of these findings is that family therapy stirs up important negative feelings in the parents that must be worked through before therapy can be considered concluded with improvement.

Langsley and Kaplan[5] used crisis family therapy for patients and their families who applied in an emergency room for psychiatric hospitalization. In all of the first 75 random experimental cases, hospitalization was avoided, compared with the control group treated by more conventional methods, all of whom were hospitalized. In addition, significant differences were found favoring the experimental group on follow-up with

Table 3
Studies of Results of Family Therapy

Study	Classification of Disturbance	No. of Cases	Results at Termination			
			Improved	Some Improvement	No Change	Worse
With Children and Adolescents						
Boughlin (1968)	Adolescent behavior problems	10	8[a]	—	2[c]	—
Freeman (1964)	Adolescent behavior problems	13[i]	11[a]	—	1	1
Kauffman (1963)	Child and adolescent behavior problems	20	21[d]	4	4[c]	—
MacGregor (1962)	Adolescent behavior problems	50[e]	43[a]	—	7[b]	—
Minuchin (1967)	Delinquent adolescents	12	7[a]	—	5	—
Safer (1966)	Child and adolescent behavior problems	29[e]	12	9[f]	8[g]	—
Sigel (1967)	Child behavior problems	19	5	9	5[h]	—

Study					
Wells (1971) Parent-child conflict	9[i]	2	4	3	—
Total Cases	171	109	26	35	1
Proportions	1.00	.64	.15	.21	—
With Adults					
Bowen (1961) Inpatient schizophrenics	7	—	3	4	—
Bowen (1961) Outpatient schizophrenics	8	1	4	3	—
Belleville (1969) Marital conflict	44	26[a]	—	18[b]	—
Carroll (1963) Outpatient neurotics	6	4	2	—	—
Fitzgerald (1969) Marital conflict	49	37	—	12	—
Pittman (1965) Adults, "work phobia"	5	5	—	—	—
Total Cases	119	73	9	37	—
Proportions	1.00	.61	.08	.31	—

From Wells R A, Dilkes T C, and Trivelli N: The results of family therapy: A critical review of the literature. Family Process, 11:189–208, 1972. (With permission.)

[a]Study only gives single "improved" category.
[b]Study combines "no change" and "worse," as "not successful."
[c]Includes cases that withdrew from treatment.
[d]Combines study categories of "considerable improvement" and "total symptomatic improvement."
[e]Evaluation is at follow-up, rather than termination.
[f]Combines study categories of "some improvement" and "partial improvement."
[g]Includes two cases reported as "symptomatic remission unrelated to therapy."
[h]Study combines "slight improvement" and "no improvement" categories.
[i]Study includes a few marital conflict cases.

respect to decreased subsequent hospitalization and earlier return to "role functioning." However, there was no difference in day-to-day functioning as measured on the Social Adjustment Inventory and a personal functioning scale. There was also little effect on long term patterns of family behavior.[19]

Wells et al.[20] have compiled two useful tables comparing outcome of family therapy with adults and with children and adolescents (Table 3). The table reveals that two-thirds of families improved and one-third did not change. (This is roughly the same rate of improvement as with individual psychotherapy.) At the very least, these results must be taken with a grain of salt as they indicate that only 2 of 290 patients got "worse."

Clinical impression and discussion with other family therapists clearly suggest that a significant number of families have problems that do not change or improve or have a structure or function that is unchanged or worse even after excellent family therapy. What the characteristics of these families are is unknown at this time, as the literature is notably lacking in descriptions of such cases.

DEFECTION AND PREMATURE TERMINATION
OF FAMILY TREATMENT

A study by Shapiro and Budman[21] has provided the first data on defection (failure of the family to appear at the first session) and premature termination of family treatment. About 30 percent of all families referred for family treatment defected and another 30 percent terminated in the first three sessions, leaving about 40 percent who continued. The main reason families gave for termination was a lack of activity on the part of the therapist, while defectors in general have had a "change of heart" and deny a problem exists. The motivation of the father appeared to play a crucial role—the more motivated he was, the more likely the family was to continue treatment.

CONCLUSION

At present, given the paucity of carefully controlled research, the relative effectiveness of family therapy cannot be accurately assessed. However, we and many others believe that it has an important clinical role. A few reports in the literature that are adequate in research design indicate that most of the families who enter family therapy will improve regardless of the type of disturbance manifested by the identified patient. However, whether that improvement persists and for how long, remains an open question. Also, the criteria for and the quality of the improvement and the treatment variables that result in improvement have yet to be evaluated. Nor have the appropriate comparisons of family therapy to other types of treatment for the same disorders been made.

As Haley[22] has pointed out, for the symptom to change, the situation should change, and evaluation measures should include not only the presence or absence of "better behavior," but also evaluation of whether or not the *system* in which the behavior took place also has changed.

REFERENCES

1. Group for the Advancement of Psychiatry. The Field of Family Psychiatry. Report No. 78. New York, Group for the Advancement of Psychiatry, 1970.
2. Mac Gregor R, Ritchie A, Serrano A, Schuster F P, Mc Danald E C, Goolishian H A: Multiple Impact Therapy With Families. New York, Mc Graw-Hill, 1964.
3. Freeman V, Klein A, Riehman L, et al: Allegheny General Hospital Study Project, Final Report. Pittsburgh, Pa, Mimeographed. 1964.
4. Friedman A, Boszormenyi-Nagy I, Jungreis J, Lincoln G, Mitchell H, Sonne J, Speck R, Spivack G: Psychotherapy for the Whole Family: Case Histories, Techniques, and Concepts of Family Therapy of Schizophrenia in the Home and Clinic. New York, Springer, 1965.
5. Langsley D, Kaplan D: The Treatment of Families in Crisis. New York, Grune & Stratton, 1968.
6. Jackson D D, Weakland, J: Conjoint family therapy. Psychiatry, 24:30–45, 1961.
7. Mac Gregor R: Multiple impact psychotherapy with families. Family Process 1:15–29, 1962.
8. Carroll E, Cambor C G, Leopold J, Miller M D, Reis W J: Psychotherapy of marital couples. Family Process, 2:25–33, 1963.
9. Greenberg I, Glick I, Match S, Riback S S: Family therapy: Indications and rationale. Arch Gen Psychiatry 10:7–25, 1964.
10. Schreiber L E: Evaluation of family group treatment in a family agency. Family Process 5:21–29, 1966.
11. Fitzgerald R V: Conjoint marital psychotherapy: An outcome and follow-up study. Family Process 8:261–271, 1969.
12. Chance E: Families in Treatment. New York, Basic Books, 1959.
13. Spiegal D, Sperber Z: Clinical experiment in short term family therapy. Paper presented at the American Orthopsychiatric Association Convention, 1967.
14. Minuchin S, Montalvo B, Guerney B G, Rosman B L, Shumer F: Families of the Slums: An Exploration of Their Structure and Treatment. New York, Basic Books, 1967.
15. Alexander J, Parsons B: Short-term behavioral intervention with delinquent

families: Impact on family process and recidivism. J Abnorm Psychol 81: 219–225, 1973.

16.   Haley J: Research on family patterns: An instrument measurement. Family Process 3:41–65, 1964.

17.   Ferreira A, Winter W: Stability of interactional variables in family decision-making. Arch Gen Psychiatry 14:352–355, 1966.

18.   Winter W: Family therapy: Research and theory, in Spielberger C D (ed): Current Topics in Clinical and Community Psychology, vol III. New York, Academic Press, 1971, pp 95–121.

19.   Flomenhaft K, Langsley D: After the crisis. Ment Hyg 55:473–477, 1971.

20.   Wells R, Dilkes T, Trivelli N: The results of family therapy. Family Process 11:189–207, 1972.

21.   Shapiro R, Budman S: Defect on, termination, and continuation in family and individual therapy. Family Process 12:55–67, 1973.

22.   Haley J: Communication and therapy: Blocking metaphors. Am J Psychotherapy 25:214–227, 1971.

14

Research on Family Process

OBJECTIVES

- To evaluate the methods, findings, and problems in the field of family process research
- To encourage further family research

This chapter is designed to enable the student to evaluate critically the literature on family process. Well over half of this literature is anecdotal, nonsystematic, uncontrolled reporting of observations that may have some value for formulation of research and clinical hypotheses.

The studies of family process to be mentioned in this chapter are those that focus mainly on the family system, rather than on the individual. Much "family" research in the past has in fact focused on the individual. Often, the identified patient reported his view of how the family was functioning, and the therapist then accepted this as factual. The individual was assumed to be a reliable, accurate informant about his own family. Such studies might include screening questionnaires about individuals, interviewing individual family members, and giving individual members projective tests. Following this, correlations to the family were made from the individual reports. Much was learned about individual family members but, more often than not, a well-rounded picture of the family unit did not emerge from such data.

Some of the papers discussed below deal with such issues as family interaction patterns, feedback systems, and rules. Others attempt to delineate factors that differentiate families with various types of disturbances from those with no evident disturbance.

ASSESSMENT OF FAMILY INTERACTION

Bodin[1] has carefully surveyed this field, and we have borrowed extensively from his outline. He has divided assessment procedures into subjective techniques and objective techniques. In subjective testing, reliance is placed on the ratings of judges who are not in the system. Objective techniques are more rigorously quantifiable and do not rely so much on ratings of judges.

Assessment can also be considered with respect to whether it assesses individual or interactional data. Some tests assess both, such as the Rorschach,[2] the Strodtbeck Revealed Differences Test,[3] and others.

For interactional studies, members of the family are brought together and the ways in which they actually deal with each other are studied. Methods include conjoint interviews in which standardized questions are asked, family therapy sessions, and task-oriented procedures, for example, games or questionnaires in which families must reconcile differences.

Subjective Techniques

There are three subtypes of subjective techniques: family tasks, family strengths inventory, and family art. For family tasks, the most efficacious approach is to set up tasks that can be quantifiably scored, such as deciding what kind of car they would like to buy if they had a given amount of money.

Another approach is to "rig" the task so that it is made more difficult for the family, for example, by asking them to distinguish different colors when the colors are made extremely difficult to distinguish; or by giving different stimuli to each member of the family without their knowing it, so it becomes impossible for them to agree (the purpose there is to see how they handle disagreement).

When pictorial apperception tests are used, the entire family can be given the test. For example, using the Thematic Apperception Test,[4] the family is given cards with visual stimuli and is asked to agree upon a story. There have been specially developed tasks for different problems, for example, cards might be specifically fitted to delinquent families. The cards have been modified for family work in that they can portray family scenes that are clearly recognizable and interesting and will engage the family to work together to produce a story.

Finally, Watzlawick[5] developed what he calls the Structured Family Interview (Appendix A) as part of a diagnostic process. A series of formal questions assesses family functioning and role structure in a step-wise fashion. This has the great advantage of being a formal, systematized way of obtaining a lot of information about the family, although at the cost of taking a moderate amount of time for gathering material that might gradually emerge in the course of therapy.

There have been several attempts to define a family strengths inventory[6] to assess healthy functions of the family in much the same way an ego strength inventory could be formulated for an individual patient. Some of the categories include developing creativity, relationships with relatives, giving encouragement, and so forth.

There are also techniques that attempt to assess family functioning through the medium of art. Day and Kwiatkowska[7] and Zierer et al.[8] have attempted to assess family dynamics using art as a shared activity for the family.

Objective Techniques

There are three subclassifications of objective techniques: techniques that rely on communication, techniques that rely on game theory, and techniques that require conflict resolution. Haley,[9,10] using a computer, has studied who speaks after whom and for how much time. This is an excellent method for objective measurement. Ravich[11] has developed a technique called "The Interpersonal Behavior Game Test" (Chapter 4, page 57).

Other procedures are based on conflict resolution. The Strodtbeck Revealed Differences Technique,[3] one of the most commonly used measures, asks subjects to make individual evaluations of a stimulus and then to reconcile any differences in interpretation that occur. Problems are set up so that only one of two possible alternatives can be used. This precludes any possibility of compromise on any given question. This procedure was modified by Ferreira,[12] who used an "unrevealed" differences technique in which the experimenter does not reveal to the family specific instances in which they disagree. Also, Ferreira allowed more availability of alternatives, giving greater assessment of more idiosyncratic thinking in families.

ASSESSMENT OF DIFFERENCES BETWEEN NORMAL AND DISTURBED FAMILIES

Hollander and Karp[13] have summarized the literature obtained from studies of more sophisticated design that contrast "normal" and "abnormal" families.

As opposed to normal families, abnormal families distribute their state-ments more evenly among family members,[14] have fewer nonlexical within-family speech similarities,[15] require more time to perform a task, are more silent, exchange less information, agree less, and fulfill each other's needs less.[16,17,18] Abnormal families exhibit significantly fewer cases of three-way alignment between father, mother, and youth and significantly greater cases of two-way align-ment between parents than do normal families.[19] Differences between normal and abnormal families have been found on several indices of power.[20,21] How-ever, no clear-cut pattern of parental dominance was reported in several other studies.[22,23] Family perceptions of adjustment and satisfaction have been used to discriminate between normal and abnormal families[24] (13, p. 814).

Delinquent versus normal comparisons indicated that in families with delin-quent children there was more parental rejection and hostility,[25] less father-son agreement and less maternal influence,[26] and more stable patterns of differential parental dominance (13, p. 815).

ASSESSMENT OF DIFFERENT TYPES
OF DISTURBED FAMILIES

This subject has been dealt with extensively in Chapter 11.

OTHER TYPES OF FAMILY RESEARCH

Two of the many other types of research are categorized here.

1. Statistical correlation studies of demographic variables are compila-tions of information on families with regard to such factors as the number of children per family, the number that are delinquent, and so forth. These factors are then correlated with other factors such as "broken homes" and "absent parents." By implication, these asso-ciations are assumed to be relevant.
2. Anthropological studies are observations of families in various cul-tures as part of a general attempt to portray the culture and examine its influence on an individual and his family. There are major prob-lems in this type of research, not the least of which is that the main informants usually are outside the family. They serve as liaison between the investigator and the families being studied. A good many studies have correlated individual personalities and child-rearing cus-toms.

PROBLEMS OF FAMILY PROCESS RESEARCH

Well-designed experiments are needed to make reliable measure-ments of typical family interactions. The ideal experiment would observe family events that can be reliably measured. Inference must be minimized. A good illustration of "hard data" is Haley's work measuring the amount of time that family members talk. Variables such as size of family, sex, and ordinal position of children, racial and cultural factors, all must be controlled. Longitudinal as well as cross-sectional studies are badly needed.

Finally, it must be restated that behavior is multicausal. Allowances for this fact must be made when evaluating what is going on; for example, are *all* the symptoms of manic-depressive disease explained by family dynamics? Can it be demonstrated that differences between normal and various types of disturbed families are significant in any causative sense? Controls must be introduced, since comparison is the essence of research. As yet, however, there are very few data on how even normal families function.

An excellent discussion of the methodological problems in family research can be found in the proceedings of a conference dealing with this topic,[27] and in Riskin and Faunce's review of family interaction research.[28]

REFERENCES

1. Bodin A: Conjoint family assessment: An evolving field, in McReynolds P (ed): Advances in Psychological Assessment, vol I. Palo Alto, Ca, Science and Behavior Books, 1968, pp 223–243.
2. Wynne L: Consensus Rorschachs and related procedures for studying interpersonal patterns. Journal of Projective Techniques and Personality Assessment 32:352–356, 1968.
3. Strodtbeck F: Husband-wife interaction over revealed differences. American Sociological Review 23:468–473, 1951.
4. Winter W D, Ferreira A J, Olson J L: Story sequence analysis of family TATs. Journal of Projective Techniques and Personality Assessment 29: 392–397, 1965.
5. Watzlawick P: A structured family interview. Family Process 5:256–271, 1966.
6. Otto H: The Otto family strength study. Graduate School of Social Work, University of Utah, Salt Lake City, Utah, 1962. Cited by Bodin A (Reference 1 this chapter).
7. Day J, Kwiatkowska H: The psychiatric patient and his well sibling: A comparison through their art productions. Bulletin of Art Therapy 2:51–66, 1962.
8. Zierer E, Sternberg D, Finn R, Farmer M: Family creative analysis: Its role in treatment. Bulletin of Art Therapy 5:47–65, 1966.
9. Haley J: Research on family patterns: An instrument measurement. Family Process 3:41–65, 1964.
10. Haley J: Speech sequences of normal and abnormal families with two children present. Family Process 6:81–97, 1967.

11. Ravich R: Game-testing in conjoint marital psychotherapy. Am J Psychother 23:217–229, 1969.

12. Ferreira A J: Decision-making in normal and pathological families. Arch Gen Psychiatry 8:68–73, 1963.

13. Hollander L Karp E: Youth psychopathology and family process research. Am J Psychiatry 130:814–817, 1973.

14. Murrell S, Stachowiak J: Consistency, rigidity, and power in the interaction of clinic and non-clinic families. J Abnorm Psychol 72:265–272, 1967.

15. Becker J, McArdle J: Non-lexical speech similarities as an index of intrafamilial identification. J Abnorm Psychol 72:408–418, 1967.

16. Ferreira A, Winter W: Family interaction and decision-making. Arch Gen Psychiatry 13:214–223, 1965.

17. Ferreira A, Winter W: Stability of interactional variables in family decision-making. Arch Gen Psychiatry 14:352–355, 1966.

18. Ferreira A, Winter W: Decision-making in normal and abnormal two-child families. Family Process 7:17–36, 1968.

19. Sackett A: Alignment patterns in normal and abnormal families. Unpublished study. Institute for Juvenile Research, Chicago, 1970.

20. Hutchinson J: Family interaction patterns and the emotionally disturbed child (abstract), in Winter W, Ferreira A (eds): Research in Family Interaction: Readings and Commentary. Palo Alto, Ca, Science and Behavior Books, 1969, pp 187–191.

21. Schuham A: Power relations in emotionally disturbed and normal family triads. J Abnorm Psychol 75:30–37, 1970.

22. Farina A, Holzberg J: Interaction patterns of parents and hospitalized sons diagnosed as schizophrenic or non-schizophrenic. J Abnorm Psychol 73:114–118, 1968.

23. Becker J, Iwakami E: Conflict and dominance within families of disturbed children. J Abnorm Psychol 74:330–335, 1970.

24. Novak A, Van der Veen F: Family concepts and emotional disturbance in the families of disturbed adolescents with normal siblings. Family Process 9:157–171, 1970.

25. Schulman R, Shoemaker D, Moelis I: Laboratory measurement of parental behavior. J Consult Psychol 26:109–114, 1962.

26. Bodin A: Family interaction: A social-clinical study of synthetic, normal, and problem family triads, in Winter W, Ferreira A (eds): Research in Family Interactions: Readings and Commentary. Palo Alto, Ca, Science and Behavior Books, 1969, pp 125–127.

27. Framo J (ed): Family Interaction. A Dialogue Between Family Researchers and Family Therapists. New York, Springer, 1972.

28. Riskin J, Faunce E: An evaluative review of family interaction research. Family Process 11:365–455, 1972.

15

Training for the Family Therapist

OBJECTIVES

- To provide the reader with an awareness of the elements of an optimum training program so that he can take steps to fill in the gaps in his own training and do better clinical work

With growing interest and experience in the field of family therapy, questions naturally arise as to how to best train family therapists. Many ideas have been promulgated and a wide range of training experiences, from the very informal to the highly structured,[1] have been established. In this chapter, some of the relevant issues will be discussed.

WHO SHOULD BE TRAINED?

Before this question can be answered, the ultimate use of the training must be clarified. Certainly, the most familiar and widespread utilization would be that of providing direct service to families in distress, along a more or less traditional counseling or psychotherapy model. These therapists may be working privately or for any one of a number of different

Some of these ideas were formulated in discussions with Arthur Bodin, Ph.D., in the summer of 1969.

institutions dealing with families in distress. A variation of this would be the use of family therapy training for those engaged in psychiatric crisis or "triage" work. They should be in a good position to evaluate the particular type of treatment needed in each instance. Such triage agents should be the best trained in a variety of disciplines and should have had considerable experience. Another growing utilization to which family therapy training is put is that of consultation to and coordination of a variety of helping agencies. In this model, the family therapist does not provide direct clinical service, but helps other workers to see and deal with family situations in a more beneficial way.

Family therapy training would appear appropriate for representatives of a number of disciplines, certainly including mental health professionals, such as psychiatrists, psychologists, psychiatric social workers, psychiatric nurses, and similar personnel. Professionals and trainees in other fields, to the extent that their work involves them to a considerable extent with families in distress, have sought and have been offered family therapy training courses. In this group are ministers, lawyers, marriage and divorce counselors for the courts, teachers, probation officers, welfare workers, physicians (especially general practitioners, "family doctors," pediatricians, obstetricians and gynecologists, and medical students[2]), and perhaps social science consultants to politicians and policy makers. With the spread of community psychiatry concepts and the increasing use of paraprofessional personnel[3,4] in a variety of helping roles, family therapy training for housewives, college students, neighborhood leaders, or "ombudsmen," and "indigenous" persons is a reality.

The question is often asked, "What sort of person makes a good family therapist?" It is impossible to give a definitive answer to the question, but certain considerations are pertinent. In general, a competent family therapist will be capable of thinking in family system terms, of empathizing with the whole family's difficulties, and of dealing actively with a complex interpersonal network. In family therapy, as in any form of treatment, the best results are obtained by those who have the best training and the most experience, knowledge, and sensitivity. It should be noted, however, that for certain families, therapists without professional degrees or prolonged formal training have been used very effectively. For example, Haley has trained black mothers, who have already raised their own children, to act as therapists for families similar to their own.

WHAT SHOULD TRAINING IN FAMILY THERAPY INCLUDE?

In an ideal world, one might say that the family therapist should have the requisite wisdom, knowledge, experience, compassion, and curiosity to do his job. More specifically, one might hope that before a person embarks on training in family therapy he would already have had experience with several "prerequisites." It would be helpful if he already knew about individual personality development, psychopathology, and psychotherapy, although usually family work will not involve as minute a dissection of intrapsychic factors as is sometimes suggested for individual treatment. It would also be helpful if he understood group dynamics and had experience in group therapy. A knowledge of the family system itself, its development over time as well as its "disorders," would obviously be germane, as would be some knowledge of larger societal systems and the mutual interaction of these with family systems.

Many structured family therapy training programs offer essentially three types of experience: seminars, clinical work, and supervision. The following outline will indicate some of the elements of a fairly complete family therapy training program. Not all of these elements will be available in any one program, nor need they necessarily be, and obviously other elements not appearing in this outline may be appropriate in a particular setting. Obviously, too, the emphasis and priorities may be quite different from one program to another.

Basic Seminars

These would be essentially discussion groups with assigned readings in relevant literature.[5]

The Family as a Social Institution

> The history of the concept of the family
> Cross-cultural family studies
> Contemporary American marriage and family
> Theories of family structure and function
> The family and other social institutions

Theories of Family Pathology

> History of the development of theories of family pathology
> Relevant variables in family pathology
> Models of family processes and family pathology
> The family system and individual pathology

Techniques of Family Evaluation and Study

> Family tests
> Interaction analysis
> Structured interviews
> Obtaining family history and family process inventory
> Formulating the family problems

Types of relevant settings and facilities
Research techniques in family systems and family treatment

Techniques of Family Therapy and Family Intervention

Historical survey of family therapy and intervention techniques
Levels of intervention
Models of intervention: prevention, service, treatment, rehabilitation
Types of family therapy
Functions, values, and goals of the family therapist
Stages of family therapy

Clinical Work

The type of exposure here obviously would have to be relevant to the trainee's goals and setting, and the particular format for the clinical work might be quite different from place to place. Although simulated families[6] and videotapes[7] may be quite helpful at times in the training experience, there is no substitute for actually sitting down with a live family and attempting to understand what is happening with them in an effort to be helpful. The following types of experiences might be included:

Intake and evaluation
Brief and crisis treatment
Extended family treatment
Family consultation to community agencies
Training in family therapy supervision

Supervision

Supervision would be designed in a variety of formats to enable the trainee to have the benefit of examining clinical experience in some organized way, and integrating it with theoretical concepts.[8] These formats might include:

Individual supervision
Intake conferences
Continuous case seminar
Treatment review
Family consultation seminar

In addition to what has been indicated above, some training directors would also include the experience of home visits and even living-in experiences with families as essential parts of a family therapy training program. The use of videotape has opened up a very helpful area, and family therapy training films are available.[9-13] Some have suggested family therapy for the family therapist's own family, as well as exploration of the therapist's own original family. Others, more modestly, have suggested that close attention be paid in supervision to helping the family therapy trainee become very aware of his own family attitudes and value systems.

Supervisors of family therapy, probably more than supervisors of other types of psychotherapy, have made extensive use of direct "on the spot" supervision. In this technique, the supervisor observes the supervisee through a one-way mirror and has direct communication with him or her via telephone or earphone. Either supervisor or trainee can interrupt the session at any time to ask questions, make suggestions, and so forth. This technique offers the advantages of timeliness, reduction of supervisee distortion of material, and on the spot relevance. Its disadvantages include being more time-consuming, sacrificing the discussion that is essential to the learning process, and having some trainees feel unduly stressed.

Another technique frequently used is role playing. A trainee will take the part of a family member and simulated families are set up using other trainees. This "experiential learning" is highly valued by some trainees, while others prefer more "cognitive" and didactic types of training, such as lectures and reading assignments.

Conferences of supervisors of family therapy training, although of uncertain value with respect to teaching effectiveness, are highly valued by those engaged in supervision. There is a feeling of camaraderie engendered, as well as an exchange of techniques of teaching.

CONTINUING EDUCATION FOR THE STUDENT
OF MARITAL AND FAMILY THERAPY

Some trainees might find it particularly valuable to use source material for more extended study in the clinical application of family therapy principles. For such students, we make the following recommendations to supplement the references already given at the ends of the chapters.

It is always useful to observe other therapists actually doing therapy, and a number of films are available. Especially interesting for their historical importance and strong personal qualities, which do not always emerge so clearly in his writings, are the films made by Ackerman.[10,11] Haley and Hoffman[14] have put together an interesting book in which appear transcripts of experienced family therapists. Included are discussions between the therapists and the authors of the book, that is, the therapists are asked what they are doing and why.

Some books that describe a family approach of a particular therapist or school might also be recommended for comparison; Satir[15] and Ackerman[16] are two of the classic examples. More recently, Ferber, Mendelsohn, and Napier,[17] and Bloch[18] have presented collections of individual papers for the student on a variety of topics concerning family therapy.

Papers of interest to family therapists appear in the journal *Family Process*, which also includes book reviews and abstracts of the current family therapy literature. A more extensive bibliography of the field can be found in the NIMH bibliography covering 1960–1964[19] and that of Glick and Haley covering 1950–1970.[20]

Part of the excitement, as well as the potential confusion, of this expanding field can be savored by being aware of and sampling current developments. In that sense we view this book as a beginning—a start in bringing together some of the major currents and trends in the field.

POST-TRAINING EDUCATION

At the conclusion of a family therapy training program, the trainee's education is actually just beginning. A good researcher, clinician, or teacher in a field that is rapidly changing like family therapy must begin a program of self-education based on a continual awareness of the literature, coursework, a willingness to evaluate his own work, and a willingness to entertain new ideas and discard old ones. As obvious as this view may seem, it is the execution of these principles that identifies the inspired and skillful clinician, teacher, or researcher.

REFERENCES

1. Sanders F, Beels C: A didactic course for family therapy trainees. Family Process 9:411–423, 1970.
2. Roeske N: The junior medical student as diagnostician of the family of an emotionally disturbed child. J Med Educ 47:51–56, 1972.
3. Hall R: A paraprofessional's view of supervision. Family Process 11:163–169, 1972.
4. Umbarger C: The paraprofessional and family therapy. Family Process 11:147–162, 1972.
5. Bodin A: Family therapy training literature: A brief guide. Family Process 8:727–779, 1969.
6. Sager C, Brayboy T, Waxenberg B: Black Ghetto Family in Therapy: A Laboratory Experience. New York, Grove Press, 1970.
7. Bodin A: Videotape applications to training family therapists. J Nerv Ment Dis 148:251–262, 1969.

8. Ferber A, Mendelsohn M: Training for family therapy. Family Process 8:25–34, 1969.
9. Family Assessment Series. 16 mm color sound film. 240 min. (Psychological Cinema Register, Pennsylvania State University, University Park, Pa., 16802).
10. In and Out of Psychosis: A Family Study. 16 mm black and white sound film, 120 min., by Nathan Ackerman, M.D. (The Family Institute, New York, NY 10021).
11. The Enemy and Myself. 16 mm black and white sound film, 50 min., by Nathan Ackerman, M.D. (The Family Institute, New York, NY 10021).
12. Family Therapy: An Introduction. 16 mm black and white sound film, 43 min., by Ira D. Glick, M.D. (University of California Medical Center, San Francisco, Ca 94143) and George J. Marshall, Sr. (Medical College of Georgia, Augusta, Ga 30904).
13. Family in Crisis. 16 mm color sound film, 48 min., by David R. Kessler, M.D. (Langley Porter Neuropsychiatric Institute, University of California San Francisco Medical Center, San Francisco, Ca 94143).
14. Haley J, Hoffman L: *Techniques of Family Therapy*. New York, Basic Books, 1967.
15. Satir V: Conjoint Family Therapy: A Guide to Theory and Technique. Palo Alto, Ca, Science and Behavior Books, 1964.
16. Ackerman N: Psychodynamics of Family Life. Diagnosis and Treatment in Family Relationships. New York, Basic Books, 1958.
17. Ferber A, Mendelsohn M, Napier A: The Book of Family Therapy. New York, Jason Aronson, 1972.
18. Bloch D (ed): Techniques of Family Psychotherapy, A Primer. New York, Grune & Stratton, 1973.
19. Family Therapy: A Selected Annotated Bibliography. Washington, D. C.: National Clearinghouse for Mental Health Information, 1965.
20. Glick I, Haley J: Family Therapy and Research. New York, Grune & Stratton, 1971.

Appendix A
The Structured Family Interview

One way of obtaining certain types of family information is that suggested by Watzlawick[1] and by Satir,[2] using a series of structured questions and tasks in family evaluation. These are used to probe certain specific variables, and also to indicate to the family, by implication, some ways of thinking about families and some areas of family life that the family members themselves may have overlooked.

This procedure has been used as an initial evaluation, and can be completed in 45 minutes to 1 hour. A one way vision-listening room may be desirable, since it allows the therapist to withdraw momentarily at appropriate points. This allows family members to work on the tasks, with the interviewer listening and observing, but not actually present.

In one of its forms, this interview consists of seven parts. The interviewer meets with the entire family, and following normal introductions, questions the family or presents them with tasks, as follows:

What is the central problem in this family at this time, in your opinion? The interviewer asks this of each family member, in turn, with all family members present. The interviewer attempts to maintain the focus on the *family problem at the present time*, rather than on one or another individual, or on past difficulties. In this first task, each family member receives an equal chance to speak, without interruption, and should get the impression that his opinions and views are worthwhile and important and will be listened to. Usually, one of the parents will be called upon first, the other parent next, and then down the line of the offspring in descending chronological order. It may be useful to consider calling first on that parent who has been less involved in family matters, or who seems more withdrawn, hesitant, passive, or weak.

The interviewer will begin to note the frames of reference that are delineated by the family members in discussing their difficulties, whether these are seen as family or individual problems, what individuals seem to be bearing the brunt of blaming, how the identified patient deals with his role, what the alliances are within the family, who seems to get interrupted by whom, who speaks for whom, who seems fearful or troubled about expressing an opinion. If he chooses, the interviewer may offer some simple statement indicating how he has understood the family members' communications, but he need not go into any extended discussion at this point. This, together with further elaboration of data gathered from the other parts of the structured interview, can be left for a separate, more extended discussion at the very end of the session or, if time is not available, it may form the basis for the second session, in which the therapist, after having had a chance to study and reflect on the data, discusses these with the family, with their implications for family difficulties and family therapy.

Plan something that family members can do together. The therapist first asks all family members together to spend a few minutes planning something that all of them would enjoy doing together. The therapist may step out of the room to observe and listen behind the one way mirror, and tell the family he will return to hear what they have planned in a few minutes. Next, the children are asked to leave the room and the marital pair are asked to plan something together that just the two of them would enjoy doing together. The interviewer again leaves the room, to return in a few minutes to hear what they have planned. Then in similar fashion, depending on the size of the family, all other family dyads and triads might be called upon in the same way. At the very least, one would want to pair the marital couple, the identified patient first with one parent, and then with the other, and other combinations as appropriate.

This task, of course, is an implicit message to the family that they should be able to interact with one another in all these combinations in mutually agreeable and satisfactory fashion. The interviewer-observer will often readily note from this section of the interview which family channels are open and which are blocked. The role-appropriateness of the interaction can be ascertained, as well as the styles of decision making. In one instance, a father and daughter working on this task came to realize that they had drifted apart, each thinking, erroneously, that the other was not interested in much mutual interaction, and neither checking this out verbally with the other over the years.

How did the two marital partners meet and decide to get married? This is asked with just the husband and wife present, and they are encouraged to elaborate at some length on the implications of this question, each one individually, and then in dialogue fashion. Not only does this tend to focus on what was most often a happier time than the present, and so serve as a useful corrective to the discouragement and frustration that one often sees when families in crisis appear for treatment the first time, but in addition may also help to clarify the mutual illusions and expectations of the "infatuation phase" and shed light on later realizations, disappointments, and patterns. It is often valuable to note the reason for and nature of the early mutual attraction and to trace the relationship through the periods of engagement, marriage, and honeymoon. (Further elaboration on this period of the family's development is given in Chapters 2 and 3.)

There often are unresolved feelings of anger, bitterness, and guilt relevant to this phase. These have served to distort or at least strongly color subsequent family developments, and they may need to be aired as part of any other attempt at family therapy. One woman poured out in great detail strong feelings of bitterness at her husband's having abandoned her for long periods during their engagement and even subsequent to their marriage, forcing her for a time to return home to live with her mother, a circumstance which her mother used as further ammunition against her daughter. In addition, the couple's sexual adjustment during the honeymoon period was very unsatisfactory. Both of these issues the wife had never discussed with her husband for fear that he would leave her altogether, since she was convinced anyway of her basic unworthiness. The strong negative feelings were never resolved and only served to sour and cripple the marriage over the years.

The parents are asked to arrive at a mutually satisfactory interpretation of a proverb which they are given, and then to call in their offspring and teach it to them. This process is, of course, particularly interesting to observe in the families of the schizophrenic patient. Their transmission of disordered thought processes, illogicality, general vagueness or meaninglessness, and/or the fact that no one has labeled this process as such, may in such families be quite striking at times (see Chapter 11).

In one instance, two parents were together able to decide on the meaning of the proverb "A rolling stone gathers no moss," although it was apparent that the mother had considerable difficulty making up her mind amongst a variety of possible meanings. When the two parents finally had agreed on a meaning and called in their daugher, a striking thing happened. The daughter, who had recently recovered after having been hospitalized for an acute schizophrenic episode, was asked by her parents what she thought the meaning of the proverb was. She responded with a variety of possible interpretations, one of which had to do with the possibility of a stone rolling uphill. The mother, at this point, instead of commenting on the unlikelihood or impossibility of such an event, commented on how interesting a possibility that was and how she herself had never thought of the meaning of the proverb in that sense, while the father kept silent.

Family members are handed slips of paper and are asked to write on it the outstanding fault of the family member seated immediately to the left. The interviewer indicates that he will write out several cards as well, based on his perceptions of some of the family members during the session so far. The cards are then collected and the therapist reads off some of the faults, one at a time, asking each family member in turn about whom in the family does the fault most apply. The therapist by the addition of his own cards can make sure that certain concepts get discussed, and can tailor the particular family traits to coincide appropriately with the particular family being dealt with. Thus, for a rather low-energy, covered-over, pseudomutual type of family, some of the faults listed were "too good," "too weak," "no enthusiasm," "doesn't speak clearly," "too sensitive to criticism," and so forth.

In this section family members are obviously given permission to be critical of one another in a protected setting, with anonymity assured. The types of faults mentioned by them, as well as the degree of unanimity or lack of unanimity with respect to the family member matched with the fault will be of considerable interest. The types of faults with which the therapist will "load" the discussion will often indicate to the family by implication that certain characteristics they may never have considered problematic or in fact may actually have considered positive attributes are here being thought of as carrying a negative connotation.

The second part of this section involves the therapist asking each family member in turn to state what he considers his own outstanding fault to be. This is often strikingly helpful in making people more thoughtful about themselves, and helps family members begin to understand each other much better. It may be the first time in their family history that they have carried on such a conversation together.

Family members are asked to write out on cards handed to them what the most admirable quality is of the family member seated immediately on their left, and the therapist also adds some cards of his own.

Again the family members are asked to try to identify the family member to whom the positive quality most applies, and the therapist will have added specific qualities to the discussion which he feels may be particularly appropriate or provocative. *Then each family member in turn will be asked to speak about what he considers his own outstanding quality.*

In addition to being able to make the same sort of correlations noted above, this section also serves to give people permission to actively consider the positive features of other family members and explicitly encourages self-respect and healthy self-assertion by asking each family member to talk about his own best quality. This sort of interaction, too, may represent a distinct breakthrough for many families.

If the identified patient is an offspring, each family member in turn is asked which of the two parents the identified patient most resembles. This section can give valuable insight into family myths, alliances, projections, and displacements.

Obviously, other specific questions will be found valuable in other circumstances, and not all of the above questions will always be equally appropriate. This type of structured interview can be made to yield valuable data at the same time that it implicitly indicates to the family areas of interest and general attitudes that the therapist deems to be important. In addition, the therapist's general manner, as well as the specific sorts of family processes that are encouraged and discouraged during the interview, will in themselves be seeds of therapeutic growth.

REFERENCES

1. Watzlawick P: A structured family interview. Family Process 5:256–271, 1966.
2. Family Interviews with Virginia Satir. Part 1. Structured Interview. 16 mm black and white sound film, 46 min., by Virginia Satir (School of Social Welfare, Educational Media Laboratory, University of California, Berkeley, Ca).

Appendix B
The Family Case History

This consists essentially of getting a detailed, narrative, longitudinal account of the family system through two or more generations (some family therapists strongly advise obtaining at least a three-generation family history), together with specific cross-sectional data relevant to the family's present characteristic modes of interaction and adaptation. This case history is in many ways analogous to the psychiatric case history and mental status examination that is traditionally utilized for individual psychiatric patients. As discussed in Chapter 4, the advantages of this sort of evaluation are that a great deal of information may be accumulated to help in trying to understand the family; that the history-gathering process itself may be quite therapeutic to the family; and that for the inexperienced therapist there is hardly any substitute for this technique if he is to become intimately familiar with what happens in a variety of families.

On the other hand, this process may be slow and cumbersome, and the gathering of voluminous data may at times serve more to confuse than to clarify the nature of the important core issues. If the family is in crisis, as it often is when coming for therapy, and if the information gathering is conducted in a mechanical, inflexible manner with little or no attention to pressing, urgent concerns, the family may become impatient and turn elsewhere for help.

The comprehensive family data outline below was utilized by the Albert Einstein College of Medicine group.[1] This is a more conceptually complex outline that the one discussed in Chapter 4, and may be useful in helping the therapist consider various frames of reference, as well as in organizing the data to indicate where some key problem areas reside.

Table 4
An Outline for Evaluating Families: Summary

Content	Conceptual Framework

I. Structure
  A. Internal
  B. External
	Thinking as a demographer

II. Individual Actors	Holistic and synthetic views: thinking as a
III. Family Themes (Content Issues)	novelist
IV. Values	
V. Role	Analytic cross sections:
VI. Communications	thinking as a social
VII. Emotions, feelings, moods	scientist
VIII. Object Relations	
IX. Development	All of the above, with a time dimension

Setting

1. What is the nature of this situation where you are learning about this family? What kinds of behavior do you expect to see in this social setting?
2. What is the overt, defined purpose of this interview in the mind of each participant?
3. What covert purposes emerge from the behavior of all participants during the interview? The interviewer-therapist has overt and covert purposes too.

AN OUTLINE FOR EVALUATING FAMILIES (IN DETAIL)

I. Structure—classifying the family on "public" dimensions

A. Internal
1. Age, sex, and relationship of household members
2. Families of origin—who are they?
3. Families of procreation—who are they?
4. Who are the current "important" family members, i.e., who is emotionally relevant to the situation under scrutiny?

B. In relation to total society
1. Ethnic group—race, national origin
2. Class—occupation, education

      3. Religion
      4. Place of residence—i.e., rural, urban

II. Individual actors: the person in center stage

    A. How does each person feel about his relationship with each other person in the family? Each member's subjective experience of his family
    B. What is that person like? An objective assessment of each individual as seen by a professional outsider

III. Family themes (shared content issues): the family in center stage

    A. Overt, what they talk about all the time, e.g., money, moving to California, father's work failure, and so forth
    B. Covert, recurrent emotionally laden themes, e.g., will we starve, can we trust one another?

IV. Values: the goals of life

    A. Family as a unit: Are the family's values congruent with those of its community, i.e., extended family, ethnic group, religion, social class?
    B. Family as a system: Are there value conflicts within the family, e.g., between the couple, across the generations?
    C. Family as a collection of individuals: Within each individual, are there value conflicts?

V. Role: what people do in social systems

    A. Family as a unit
        1. Relation to the economy—give labor, get goods, have assets
        2. Relation to polity—give loyalty, get leadership
        3. Relation to community—give participation, get support
    B. Family as a system
        1. Major internal structures
           a. Coalition between the parents
           b. Boundary between sexes
           c. Boundary between generations
        2. Characteristic subgroups
           a. Coalitions (working alliances)
           b. Pairings (loving couples)
           c. Splits (persistent hostilities)

C. Family as a collection of individuals
    1. Husband as leader, lover, provider
       Father as nurturer, disciplinarian, companion
    2. Wife as follower, lover, nurturer
       Mother as nurturer, disciplinarian, companion
    3. Each child in age, sex appropriate roles

VI.   Communication: the "how" of meaningful behavior
Two basic kinds of information: what's new—the information about novel events; what's usual—the information about the static properties of the system, definition of constant relationships

A. Family as a unit
    1. Channel: How much of the two basic kinds of information in each channel?
       a. Lexical
       b. Paraverbal
       c. Movement, gesture, posture, facial expression
       d. Action—being present or absent, hitting, bribing
    2. Clarity: Does each message focus and become clear or does it become tangential (i.e., change into something else) or amorphous (i.e., dissolve into nothing)? A focus on the fate of a message through time
    3. Congruence: Are the many messages about the same topic (there are always several) congruent with each other? This refers to the logical structure of the messages and their sequences (e.g., denial, double binds)
B. Family as a system: For each dyad
    1. Relative degree to which that dyad is complementary or symmetrical
    2. Degree of overtness and covertness. How much do these people take responsibility for their messages to each other. Refers to A2 and A3
C. Family as a collection of individuals: Each person may be assessed as a sender and receiver of information, utilizing the dimensions of A and B

VII. Emotions, feelings, moods

A. Family as a unit
    1. Typical moods, emotional climate
    2. What are the boundaries, the limits of feeling, in this family? What is *not* allowed or feared?
    3. How much contagion of anxiety and depression? How dealt with?

     B.   Family as a system. Examine each dyad in the family on the three polarities:
1. Accept-Reject
2. Dominate-Submit
3. Love-Hate
Are there any concealed three-person systems as revealed by feelings of jealousy and envy?
     C.   Family as individuals
Refer back to II, Individual Actors

VIII. Object relations
In an existential sense, how are the family members related to the family and to each other? The following is a descending scale from mature to immature:
     A.   Mature—Self differentiated from other; other seen for his own qualities; relatedness present
     B.   Transference—Self differentiated from other; other seen as if he were someone else, usually a member of self's family of origin; relatedness present
     C.   Projection of "good me"—Self not differentiated from other; other seen as if he were someone else, the embodiment of self-valued qualities; self often feels he lacks enough of these qualities and would like more of them; relatedness present
     D.   Projection of "bad me"—Self not differentiated from other; other seen as if he were someone else, the embodiment of self's hated qualities; self usually does not acknowledge that self possesses these qualities; relatedness present
     E.   Fusion-Merger—Self and other not differentiated; contagion of affects with no "motive" for the feeling prominent; relatedness present
     F.   Self-relatedness—Relatedness absent. Self involved with self alone; other seen solely in terms of need gratifying or frustrating properties
All six modes of relatedness are seen in almost all families. It is the quantitative preponderance that is crucial.

IX. Developmental history through time

     A.   Normative crises—the significant turning points each family must experience
1. First meeting of parents
2. Engagement
3. Marriage
4. Birth of children (especially first)
5. Children starting school

      6. Children beginning adolescence
      7. First child leaving the home
      8. Last child leaving the home
      9. Retirement of major wage earner
    10. Death of spouse
 B. Nonnormative crises
      1. Internal: Deaths, illnesses, separations and additions of other members to family
      2. External: Major employment shifts, war, flood, moving

REFERENCE

1.   Ferber A, Mendelsohn M: Personal communication.

Author Index

Subject Index

a
4 b
5 c
6 d
7 e
8 f
9 g
0 h
1 i
8 2 j